6/01

# CABINS, COTTAGES & VILLAS

## Enchanting Homes for Mountain, Sea or Sun

# THE "CAPRINI" VILLA
## INSPIRED BY
### *danielle* SATER

*W*ell acquainted with the world of architecture, Danielle Sater painted a dream home, translated by Dan into a work that's designed for the real world. To view floor plans, see page 121.

*danielle sater*

# CABINS, COTTAGES & VILLAS

## *Enchanting Homes for Mountain, Sea or Sun*

Sater*Design*

COLLECTION

HOME PLANNERS
TUCSON, ARIZONA

**Published by Home Planners, LLC**

A Division of Hanley-Wood, LLC

Editorial and Corporate Offices:

3275 West Ina Road, Suite 110

Tucson, Arizona 85741

**Distribution Center:**

29333 Lorie Lane

Wixom, Michigan 48393

**Patricia Joseph,** President

**Jan Prideaux,** Editor in Chief

**Nick Nieskes,** Project Plans Editor

**Ashleigh Muth,** Text

*Editor*  Laura Hurst Brown

*Designer*  Matthew S. Kauffman

Illustrated by Dave Jenkins

Photography by ©Laurence Taylor:

  Page *ii*, Dan and Danielle Sater

  Back flap, Dan Sater

First Printing, March 2001

10 9 8 7 6 5 4 3 2 1

Printed in the United States of America

Library of Congress Catalog Card Number: 00-134234

ISBN softcover: 1-881955-73-7

*Mount Julian,*
*page 28*

# Contents

*Santa Rosa,
page 54*

RUGGED

RUGGED STONE

A SENSE OF *nature*

STIR THE SOUL

*stir the soul*

# CABINS

Laurel Ridge

*Design © The Sater Group*

This fabulous mountain home begins with a stunning transom, which tops a classic paneled door and sets off a host of windows brightening the facade. A grand entry leads to a glorious two-story foyer that grants views through the rear of the home to the spacious veranda. A three-sided fireplace and wet bar invites entertaining on any scale, grand or cozy.

The formal dining room features its own access to the veranda. An open arrangement of the interior allows the cook to enjoy the company of guests, and easily prepare a meal in a well-equipped kitchen. A wide window overlooks the outdoor kitchen area of the patio, which includes a rinsing sink and outdoor grill. Nearby, a secondary bedroom adjoins a full bath and can be converted to guest quarters.

An upper level dedicated to the owners retreat boasts a wide deck where, on a clear day, one may see forever. The beauty of natural light splashes the master bedroom with a sense of the outdoors and mingles with the crackle of the fireplace. Private baths for two owners provide separate amenities, including an exercise area and a knee-space vanity. Separate garages on the lower level lead to an entry vestibule with both an elevator and stairs.

## PLAN HPT030001

Main Level: 2,039 square feet

Upper Level: 1,426 square feet

Lower-level Entry: 374 square feet

Total Living Area: 3,839 square feet

Width: 56'-0"

Depth: 54'-0"

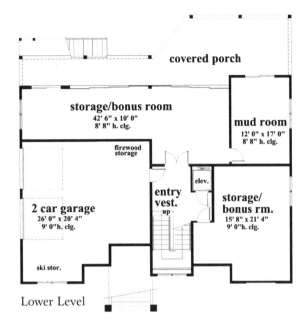

Lower Level

Main Level

## ART NOUVEAU

*Fine details bring out the best in the rich character of this design, with all the charm of a country home.*

Upper Level

Design © The Sater Group

## Buckhurst Lodge

Asymmetrical gables, classic details and a bold mix of textures create an intriguing interplay of rustic and refined elements in this stately cabin. An upper portico defined by double columns and an arched cover echoes the entry. A mid-level foyer with a stylish staircase eases the transition from ground level to an open arrangement of the grand living and dining areas. Built-ins, French doors and a hearty fireplace define the great room, which boasts a vaulted ceiling. Guests will find the covered porch and deck on balmy evenings, and appreciate the hearth when the weather's chilly.

Planned events are a cinch when the formal dining room connects with a well-organized kitchen. Wrapping counters, an angled double sink and ample storage give the culinary artist an easy environment in which to create a meal—whether it's a sit-down dinner or a quick bite. Natural light comes into the area from windows in the dining room and kitchen, creating an appealing space that's just right for any occasion.

The upper level is dedicated to the master suite—an open rambling area with plenty of room for luxury. With generous outdoor views and a private porch, a homeowner could be persuaded to just sit and watch the sunset awhile—never mind the honks and beeps of city life.

### PLAN HPT030002

Main Level: 1,383 square feet

Upper Level: 595 square feet

Total Living Area: 1,978 square feet

Width: 48'-0"

Depth: 42'-0"

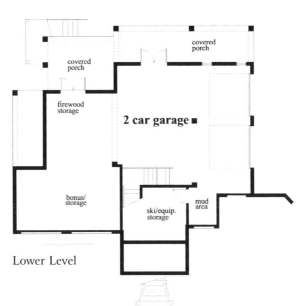

Lower Level

## PERFECT PIED-A-TERRE

*Open-air porches and roomy decks extend the living areas of this ideal getaway. Plenty of French doors blur the lines between indoors and out, and really bring in the light*

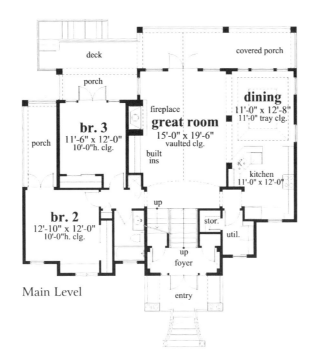

Main Level

Upper Level

Walden Hill

Design © The Sater Group

Towering gables with matchstick details announce a positively stunning entry, which boasts sets of square columns and simple balustrades. An interior staircase leads from the foyer to a spacious great room, made inviting by a fireplace and French doors to a rear wraparound porch.

An open arrangement of the formal dining room, kitchen and great room provides a flexible space that's just right for any occasion, planned or casual. Guests may linger outdoors after dinner to catch some cool breezes or wish on a star.

The left wing of the plan is dedicated to the master suite, which boasts access to a private area of the back porch. A tray ceiling sets off the owners bedroom and complements the natural light of two windows. The private bath features a walk-in closet, garden tub and oversized shower.

Upstairs, two guest suites lead to an open deck and covered porches, enabling wide views and breezy living space for family members or guests. A loft area enjoys an overlook to the great room and the entry foyer.

## PLAN HPT030003

Main Level: 1,510 square feet

Upper Level: 864 square feet

Total Living Area: 2,374 square feet

Bonus Space: 810 square feet

Width: 44'-0"

Depth: 49'-0"

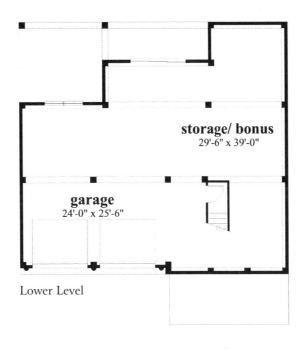

Lower Level

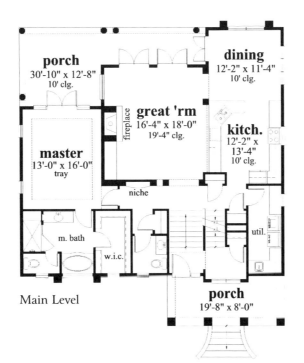

Main Level

# HAPPY HAVEN

*Dressed with the deft touches usually found in much larger homes, this rustic cabin is one of a kind.*

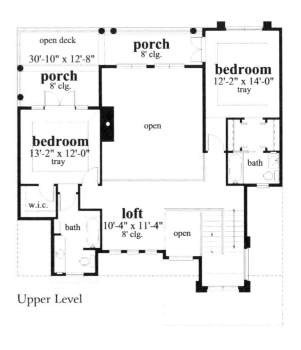

Upper Level

Whisperwood

Design © The Sater Group

The horizontal lines and straightforward details of this rustic plan borrow freely from the Arts and Crafts style, remembered with a dash of traditional warmth. Gallery porches open the indoors to nature, and classy windows add plenty of wide views. An intelligent arrangement of rooms provides both formal and casual living space to the left of the plan.

Clustered sleeping quarters ramble across the opposite side of the main level, while the kitchen and nook at the heart of the home bring people together for easy meals and conversation. The homeowner's retreat is all decked out with a wall of glass, two walk-in closets and generous dressing space.

Designed for a narrow lot, the house takes full advantage of the land with a lower level that sprawls across the entire footprint. From ski storage to a room-sized bin for firewood, this level offers plenty of flexibility. A spacious mud area opens through sets of French doors to a covered porch that's perfect for watching fireflies glimmer. Bonus space easily converts to a hobby room. The two-car garage leaves plenty of space for bicycles.

## PLAN HPT030004

Total Living Area: 2,137 square feet
Width: 44'-0"
Depth: 63'-0"

# HIGH PRAIRIE

*Modish details connect past and future with an easy charm and striking details that conceal a hardworking interior.*

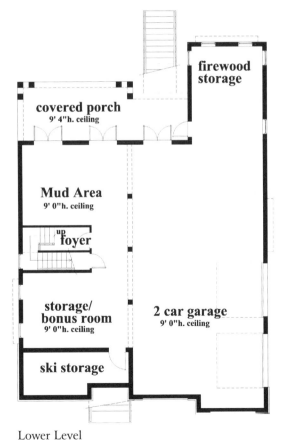

Lower Level

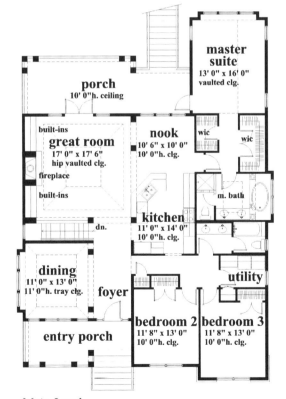

Main Level

*Design © The Sater Group*

## Cascade Ridge

W himsical and powerful, this rugged elevation blends regional influences with a powerful statement of style. Chic stickwork and a hip roof complement a dramatic mix of stone, shingles, horizontal siding and a slate roof. Doric columns frame the entry and announce an interior that's both wide open and well defined. A mid-level foyer and covered entry porch ease the transition from ground level to living space.

Inside, steps lead down to the great room, which boasts a two-story ceiling detailed with exposed spiderbeams. Three sets of French doors open to the covered veranda while a massive fireplace, flanked by built-in shelves, and windows further define the space. A gourmet kitchen features a centered cooktop island counter, walk-in pantry and a pass-through shared with the great room. Nearby, the formal dining room provides a tray ceiling and a stunning bay window that brings in a sense of nature.

An upper-level loft boasts impressive arches overlooking the great room. The loft not only offers space for computers and books, it connects two secondary bedrooms. Bedroom 3 opens to a sun deck—the perfect place for enjoying the great outdoors.

## PLAN HPT030005

Main Level: 2,096 square feet

Upper Level: 892 square feet

Total Living Area: 2,988 square feet

Bonus Space: 1,295 square feet

Width: 56'-0"

Depth: 54'-0"

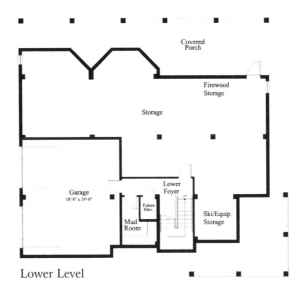

Lower Level

Main Level

## POWERFUL SURROUNDINGS

*Double columns, an arch-top transom and glass panels provide plenty of reasons to linger on the front porch but the interior vistas are even grander.*

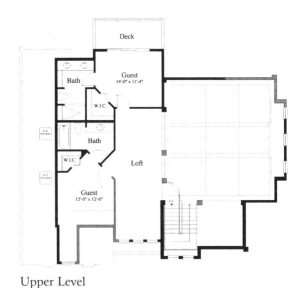

Upper Level

Berkeley Square

*Design © The Sater Group*

An array of elegant details create a wonderful welcoming entry to this new-century home, with massive stone pillars, a matchstick pediment and stunning turret. The mid-level foyer leads up to the spacious living area and down to the lower-level bonus room, which boasts a covered porch, ski storage, a mud room and a three-car garage.

On the main level, a vaulted ceiling highlights the great room, and a fireplace warms the open interior. French doors bring in a feeling of nature and provide access to the rear covered porch. Formal rooms open from the central hall and include a study that's secluded behind pocket doors.

Secondary sleeping quarters reside to the right of the plan, connected by a gallery hall that offers a full bath, a laundry and linen storage. Bedroom 3 features a window seat and a lovely set of French doors that open to the rear porch.

Upstairs, a rambling master suite enjoys a luxury bath with separate vanities, a whirlpool tub framed by windows, and a walk-in closet with dressing space. The owners bedroom provides a private porch and a sitting area.

## PLAN HPT030006

Main Level: 1,671 square feet

Upper Level: 846 square feet

Lower-level Entry: 140 square feet

Total Living Area: 2,657 square feet

Width: 44'-0"

Depth: 55'-0"

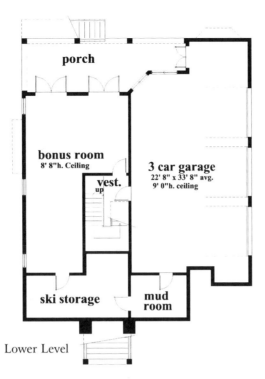

Lower Level

# CENTER STAGE

*Elegant muntin windows set off a show-stopping pediment entry that says "welcome home."*

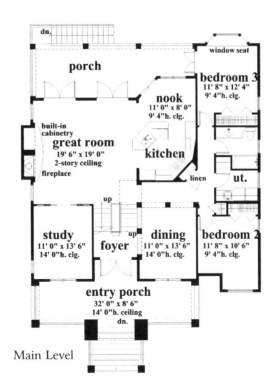

Main Level

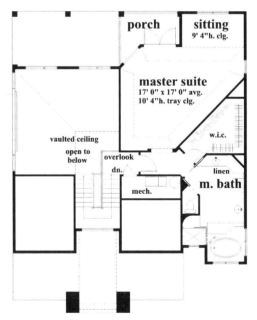

Upper Level

Stone Bridge

*Design © The Sater Group*

Constructed of stone and siding, this exuberant retreat begins with a grand entry and a pleasing mix of smooth classic columns and rustic balustrades. A vaulted gable that points toward heaven introduces this luxurious plan and provides an eye-catching exterior. Throughout the home, the creative use of arches and open space complements tall windows, which brighten the rooms with daylight. French doors open the great room to the outside, extending the living space. Access to the wraparound veranda to the rear of the plan adds a natural touch to the owners wing and the formal dining room.

The master suite opens through a graceful archway from the central gallery hall. A wall of glass frames a rather ideal space that can serve as a sitting area. A soaking tub features views of a side garden, while the step-up shower boasts glazed glass-block windows. A separate entrance leads to the quiet study, which is highlighted by a tray ceiling and defined by built-in bookshelves and richly detailed cabinetry. This room is brightened by a tall window that overlooks the front property.

## PLAN HPT030007

Main Level: 1,798 square feet

Upper Level: 900 square feet

Total Living Area: 2,698 square feet

Width: 54'-0"

Depth: 57'-0"

# GREAT OUTDOORS

*A breezy front porch invites lingering and announces a home that's carefully crafted to allow a sense of nature and provide powerful views.*

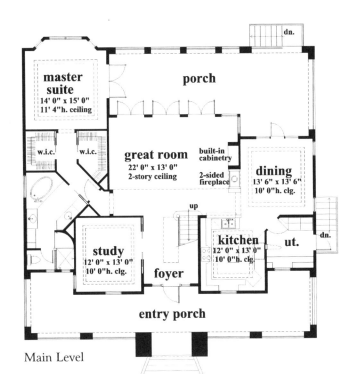

Main Level

Upper Level

Wedgewood

*Design by The Sater Group*

Matchstick details and a careful blend of stone and siding lend a special style and spirit to this stately retreat. Multi-pane windows take in the scenery and deck out the refined exterior of a cabin-style home designed for a life of luxury. An open foyer shares its natural light with the great room, a bright reprieve filled with its own outdoor light. Dinner guests may wander from the coziness of the hearth space into the crisp night air through lovely French doors.

The homeowner's retreat is an entire wing of the main level. Tall windows flank a glass door that opens from the master bedroom to a private porch, where cool mountain breezes stir the senses. A generous dressing area provides a walk-in closet and additional linen storage. Special amenities in the bath include an oversized shower and garden tub. Upper-level sleeping quarters bring together two gorgeous bedrooms with plenty of outdoor views. A spacious full bath in the central hall also serves a loft area that's great for computers and books.

## PLAN HPT030008

Main Level: 1,342 square feet

Upper Level: 511 square feet

Total Living Area: 1,853 square feet

Width: 44'-0"

Depth: 40'-0"

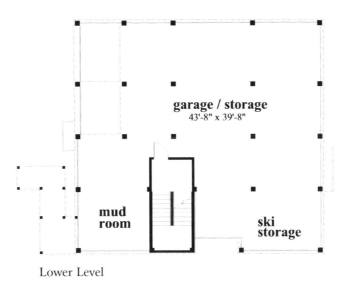

garage / storage
43'-8" x 39'-8"

mud room

ski storage

Lower Level

# ARTS AND CRAFTS

*A trendy transom and glass panels call up an extraordinary era with a look that's great in any neighborhood.*

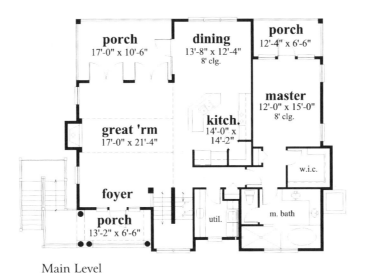

porch
17'-0" x 10'-6"

dining
13'-8" x 12'-4"
8' clg.

porch
12'-4" x 6'-6"

great 'rm
17'-0" x 21'-4"

kitch.
14'-0" x 14'-2"

master
12'-0" x 15'-0"
8' clg.

w.i.c.

foyer

util.

m. bath

porch
13'-2" x 6'-6"

Main Level

open deck
17'-0" x 10'-6"

bedroom
13'-8" x 12'-0"
12' clg.

open

loft

bath

bedroom
10'-0" x 13'-2"
12' clg.

Upper Level

Chanteclair

Design © The Sater Group

A row of transom windows really brings in the light and decks out the entry of this rustic design. With a rugged blend of stone and siding, an inviting mix of details creates the kind of comfortable beauty that every homeowner craves. Massive stone columns support a striking pediment entry, which leads up to the dazzling main-level landing and great room.

A spacious formal dining room complements a gourmet kitchen designed to serve any occasion, equipped with a walk-in pantry and a nearby powder room. The morning nook boasts a wall of glass that allows casual diners to kick back and be at one with nature.

Separate sleeping quarters thoughtfully places the master suite to the right of the plan, in a wing of the home that includes a private porch. A lavish private bath provides a retreat for the fortunate homeowner, with two walk-in closets, a garden tub and oversized shower. Guest suites on the opposite side of the plan share a hall with a staircase that leads to a lower-level mudroom, porch and ski storage.

## PLAN HPT030009

Total Living Area: 2,430 square feet
Width: 70'-2"
Depth: 53'-0"

# ART OF THE COUNTRY
*Matchstick details play against rugged blends of stone and siding and refined rows of muntin windows.*

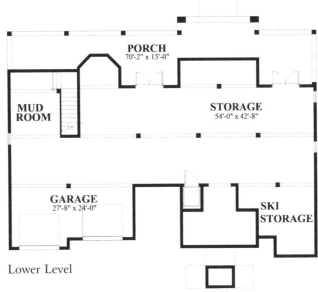

Lower Level

Main Level

Hampshire Ridge

Design © The Sater Group

The Sater Design Collection

A magnificent turret provides a great accent to the well-crafted look of this historic exterior. Architectural details and timeless materials announce a relaxed interior with comfy niches and grand open spaces. The foyer staircase leads up to a landing that introduces the home and offers a nearby powder room. French doors open the main-level living areas to the outside, and allow fresh mountain air to waft through unrestrained rooms that own a sense of comfort. Built-in cabinetry frames the massive fireplace, which warms the decor and atmosphere. Window seats invite readers and thinkers to settle down for a while.

Arches and columns help define the interior space, lending a sense of privacy to the dining area—a stunning space with views and access to the covered porch. A space-saving kitchen provides a food-preparation island and wrapping counters. On the upper level, two secondary bedrooms share a full bath that includes an oversized shower. Double doors lead to the master retreat, which opens to a private area of the porch and includes a compartmented bath with an oversized shower.

## PLAN HPT030010

Main Level: 874 square feet

Upper Level: 880 square feet

Lower-level Foyer: 242 square feet

Total Living Area: 1,996 square feet

Width: 34'-0"

Depth: 43'-0"

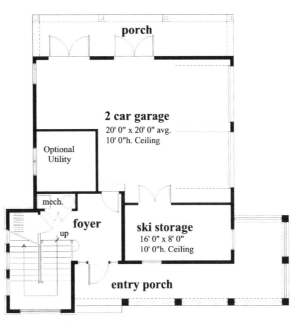

Lower Level

# AMERICAN TREASURE

*A period piece with an easy spirit fits any place with familiar charm.*

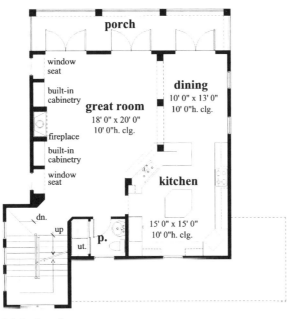

Main Level

Upper Level

Mount Julian

*Design © The Sater Group*

This traditional country cabin is a vacationer's dream. Stone and vertical wood siding deck out the rustic exterior, while the interior amenities surround the homeowner in lavish style. An elegant entry extends to the foyer, where straight ahead, the two-story great room visually expands the lofty interior. This room provides a warming fireplace and offers built-in cabinetry.

Double doors open to a fresh veranda, which wraps around to the rear deck—a perfect place to enjoy the outdoors. The dining room opens through double doors to the veranda on the left side of the plan, while the kitchen offers an efficient pantry on the right.

A family bedroom with a private bath resides on the main floor, along with a powder room and laundry. Upstairs, a vaulted ceiling enhances the master suite and a sumptuous bath. A private deck from the master suite can be accessed through a set of double doors. The loft area overlooking the great room accesses a second deck. Two porches open on either side of the bonus room for additional outdoor space.

## PLAN HPT030011

Main Level: 1,143 square feet

Upper Level: 651 square feet

Total Living Area: 1,794 square feet

Width: 32'-0"

Depth: 57'-0"

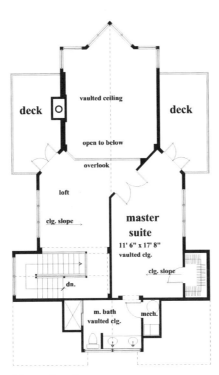

Upper Level

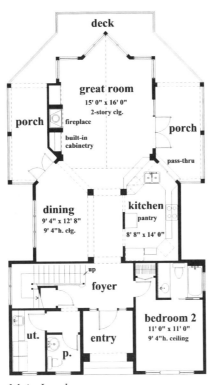

Main Level

# A WAY OF LIFE

*Grand views and open spaces own beauty without surrendering practicality or comfort.*

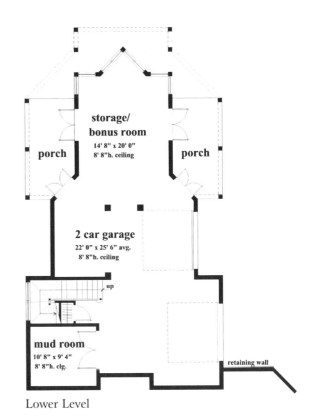

Lower Level

New Waterford

Design © The Sater Group

Tall windows and a lofty deck bestow spectacular views across the front of this rustic hideaway—perfect for any region. The wraparound porch extends the living and dining space to the soul-stirring beauty of the outdoors. A beam ceiling highlights the great room, creating a pleasing mix of style and warmth.

An innovative arrangement of interior space allows natural light to brighten the kitchen through the broad windows of the breakfast bay. A food-preparation island and walk-in pantry extend the facility of the kitchen, which easily serves occasions, planned or casual. Nearby, an ample utility area leads to a side staircase. A powder room is placed just off the foyer.

Upper-level sleeping quarters include two secondary bedrooms, which share a compartmented bath. The master suite features a handsome bedroom with a vaulted sitting bay and a two-sided fireplace shared with the bath. French doors open to a wraparound balcony and deck, where a relaxed attitude is *de rigueur* and shoes are definitely optional.

## PLAN HPT030012

Main Level: 1,266 square feet

Upper Level: 1,324 square feet

Total Living Area: 2,590 square feet

Width: 34'-0"

Depth: 63'-2"

# FINE LINES

*The richly detailed angles and gentle mix of rustic and smooth materials richly embellish this elegant-yet-casual retreat.*

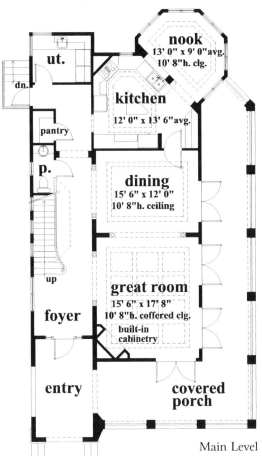

Main Level

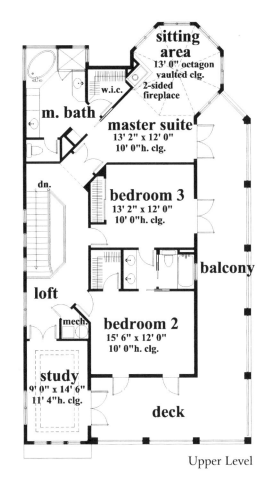

Upper Level

Design © The Sater Group

Lake Tahoe

Stonework and elements of Craftsman style make a strong statement but are partnered here with a sweet disposition. The grand entry porch provides ample space for appreciating the night sky or just taking in the sights and sounds of nature. Sidelights and transoms enrich the elevation and offer a warm welcome to a well-accoutered interior with up-to-the-minute amenities.

A wealth of windows allows gentle breezes to flow through the living space, and French doors extend an invitation to enjoy the rear covered porch. The great room can handle the powerful views, with an extended-hearth fireplace and built-in cabinetry to create a downright comfortable place to kick off one's shoes and stay awhile. Nearby, a well-organized kitchen offers a pass-through to the great room, and service to the formal dining room through a convenient butler's pantry.

Upstairs, the master suite sports a private sitting area that opens to an upper deck through French doors. The upper-level gallery provides an overlook to the great room and connects the owners retreat with a secondary bedroom that opens to the deck.

## PLAN HPT030013

Main Level: 1,542 square feet
Upper Level: 971 square feet
Total Living Area: 2,513 square feet
Width: 46'-0"
Depth: 51'-0"

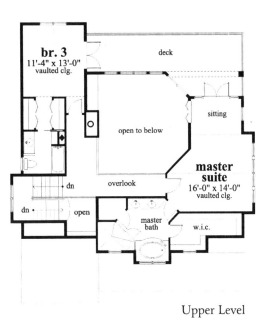

Upper Level

# IN THE DETAILS

*Rugged stone and Craftsman details make a happy marriage on this elevation, decked out with stunning fanlight transoms.*

Main Level

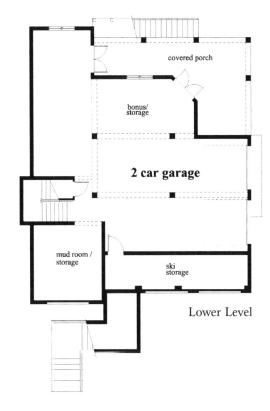

Lower Level

Design © The Sater Group

**Albert Ridge**

Dramatic rooflines complement a striking arched-pediment entry and a variety of windows on this refined facade. The entry porch leads to a landing that rises to the main-level living area—an arrangement well suited for unpredictable climates. A fireplace warms the great room, which sports a tray ceiling and opens to the rear porch through lovely French doors. This mid-level outdoor space presents an opportunity to enjoy the benefits of a natural environment.

In the heart of the home, the gourmet kitchen serves a stunning formal dining room, which offers wide views through a wall of windows. Separate sets of French doors let in natural light and fresh air, and permit access to both of the rear porches. A guest bath and a convenient laundry are nearby.

The private master suite enjoys a coffered ceiling, walk-in closet and private access to one of the rear porches. The bath provides a garden tub, two-sink vanity and linen storage. A grand central staircase leads to the upper-level sleeping quarters and offers a splendid window that brings sunlight indoors. The gallery hall on this level leads to a crow's nest—a contemplative space just right for reading or watching the world go by.

## PLAN HPT030014

Main Level: 1,537 square feet

Upper Level: 812 square feet

Total Living Area: 2,349 square feet

Width: 45'-4"

Depth: 50'-0"

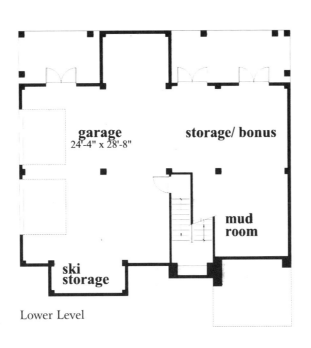

Lower Level

# BRAVE NEW WORLD

*Out-of-sight features such as an up-there crow's nest and web-surfing loft create ultra-new digs ready for the future.*

Main Level

Upper Level

Sierra Canyon

Design © The Sater Group

Climate is a key component of any mountain retreat, and outdoor living is an integral part of its design. This superior cabin features open verandas and covered porches, creating enjoyable environments—no matter what the weather. A bang-up-to-date mix of matchstick details and rugged stone set off this lodge-house facade, concealing a well-defined interior.

An interactive floor plan encourages conversation in the great room, dining room and outdoor areas. Windows line the breakfast bay and brighten the kitchen, which features a center cooktop island and a walk-in pantry. A door leads out to a covered patio, a summer kitchen with a built-in grill, and, on the other side of the plan, a veranda with a cabana bath.

The upper level features a secluded master suite with a spacious bath that rambles around the bedroom, beginning with a double walk-in closet and ending with a garden view of the veranda. A two-sided fireplace extends warmth to the whirlpool spa-style tub and to the owners bedroom. Sliding glass doors lead outside, where gentle breezes invigorate the senses.

## PLAN HPT030015

Main Level: 2,391 square feet

Upper Level: 1,539 square feet

Lower-level Entry: 429 square feet

Total Living Area: 4,359 square feet

Width: 71'-0"

Depth: 69'-0"

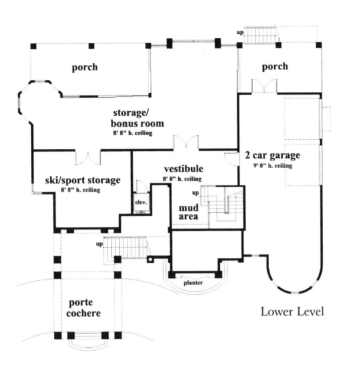

Lower Level

# NEW BALANCE

*An inviting mix of exquisite textures, soothing colors and natural wood draws a fine line between home and nature.*

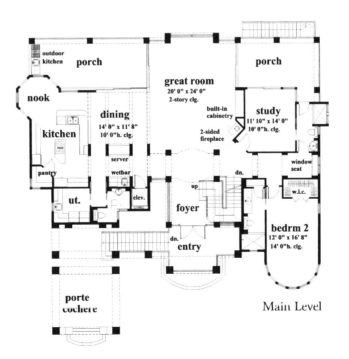

Main Level

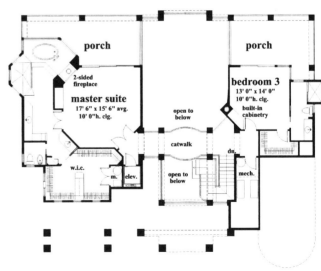

Upper Level

Weymouth Inn

*Design © The Sater Group*

With a flair for perfection, this dream cabin captures the finest historic details in rooms furnished with comfort and style. A grand foyer features a radius staircase that decks out the entry hall and defines the wide-open interior. A formal dining room is served through a butler's pantry by a kitchen so well equipped, a culinary artist would feel at home here. Casual space includes a leisure room that sports a corner fireplace, tray ceiling and built-in media center. Fling open the French doors and let the sunshine in. An outdoor kitchen makes it easy to enjoy life outside on the wraparound porch.

The main-level master suite is suited with a spacious bedroom, two walk-in closets, and a lavish bath with separate vanities and a bumped-out whirlpool tub. A bay window in the bedroom boasts wide views that extend beyond a private porch.

Upstairs, two family bedrooms share a compartmental bath, and a guest suite boasts a roomy bath and ample wardrobe space. A computer center, linen area and a loft overlooking the grand foyer complete the second floor.

# HERE AT HOME

*With an oh-so-beautiful facade, this rustic design boasts ultra-comfortable rooms that invite a sense of joie de vivre.*

## PLAN HPT030016

Main Level: 2,083 square feet

Upper Level: 1,013 square feet

Total Living Area: 3,096 square feet

Width: 52'-0"

Depth: 88'-0"

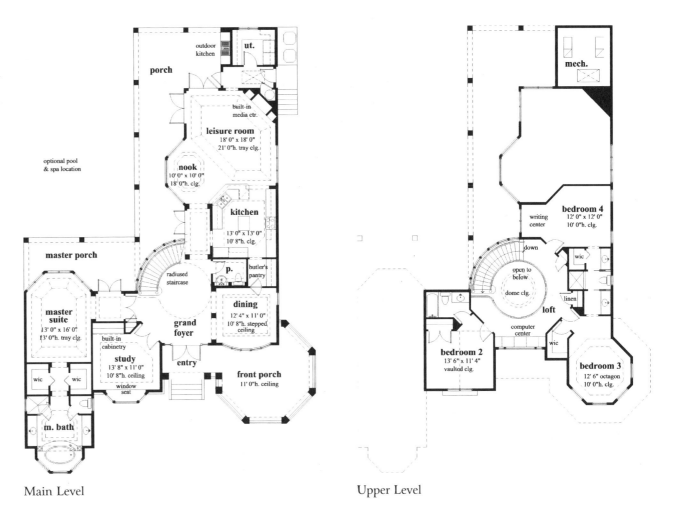

Main Level

Upper Level

Design © The Sater Group

## Bradley House

The Sater Design Collection

This luxurious vacation cabin is the perfect rustic paradise, whether set by a lake or a mountain scene. The wrap-around entry porch is friendly and inviting. Double doors open to the foyer, which is flanked by the study with built-in cabinetry and the formal dining room.

The octagonal great room features a multi-faceted vaulted ceiling that illuminates the interior. This room offers a fireplace, a built-in entertainment center and three sets of double doors, which lead to a vaulted porch. The gourmet island kitchen is brightened by a bayed window and a pass-through to the porch.

Two walk-in closets and a whirlpool bath await to lavish the homeowner in the master suite. A set of private double doors open to the vaulted master porch. The U-shaped stairway leads to a loft that overlooks the great room and the foyer. Two family bedrooms with private baths are featured upstairs. A computer center, a morning kitchen and a second-floor deck are located at the end of the hall.

## PLAN HPT030017

Main Level: 1,855 square feet

Upper Level: 964 square feet

Total Living Area: 2,819 square feet

Width: 66'-0"

Depth: 50'-0"

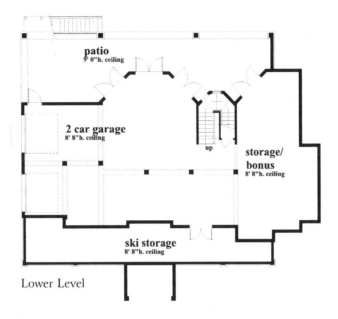

Lower Level

## ELEMENTS OF STYLE

*Detailed glass panels and horizontal lines speak softly of the Prairie style with a twist of future dash.*

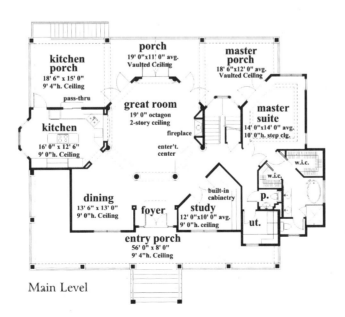

Main Level

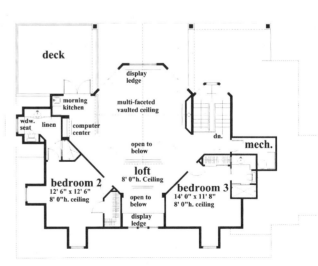

Upper Level

Design © The Sater Group

## Wolf Summit

Tall windows wrap this noble exterior with dazzling details and allow plenty of natural light inside. A wraparound porch sets a casual but elegant pace for the home, with space for rockers and swings. Well-defined formal rooms are placed just off the foyer, which also leads to a wide-open great room. A host of French doors open this space to an entertainment veranda and, of course, inspiring views.

Even formal meals take on the ease and comfort of a mountain region in the stunning, open dining room. Three large windowpanes display gorgeous outdoor views and bring in plenty of daylight as well as moonglow. Nearby, a gourmet kitchen packed with amenities is prepared to serve any occasion.

The master wing includes a private hall that provides a powder room. Nearby, a vestibule with linen storage leads to a study that also opens back to the foyer. A tray ceiling and wide bay window enhance the owners bedroom, and a dressing area framed by walk-in closets leads to the lavish bath. Two secondary suites, each with a spacious bath and walk-in closet, share a catwalk on the upper level.

## PLAN HPT030018

Main Level: 2,146 square feet
Upper Level: 952 square feet
Lower-level Entry: 187 square feet
Total Living Area: 3,285 square feet
Width: 52'-0"
Depth: 65'-4"

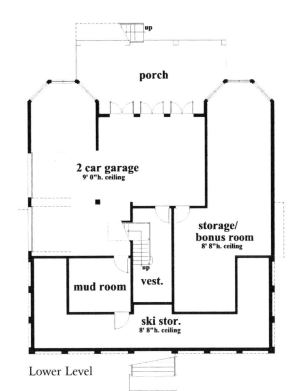

Lower Level

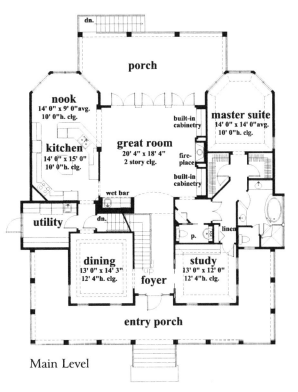

Main Level

# A PLACE IN SPACE

*Wild mountain breezes invigorate the senses in the great outdoor living areas of this sensational retreat.*

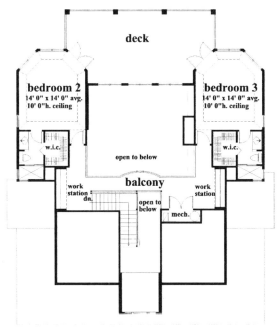

Upper Level

Design © The Sater Group

## Trail Ridge

This trendy cabin is the ideal vacation home for a retreat to the mountain lake—or the perfect everyday getaway for an Arcadian suburb. A stone and siding exterior blends well into any scene. Inside, beyond the covered front porch, the foyer steps lead up to the formal living areas on the main floor.

The study is enhanced by a vaulted ceiling and double doors, which open to the front balcony. This room is a perfect home office for quiet escapes. A utility room, located to the right, also opens to the front balcony.

Vaulted ceilings create a spacious feel throughout the home, especially in the central great room, which overlooks the rear deck—perfect for summertime entertainment. The gourmet island kitchen is open to an adjacent breakfast nook.

Guest quarters are provided on the right side of the plan—one boasts a private bath, while the other has access to the full hall bath. The master suite is thoughtfully placed on the left side of the plan for privacy and offers two walk-in closets and a pampering whirlpool master bath. Storage space abounds in the basement, alongside the two-car garage.

## PLAN HPT030019

Main Level: 2,385 square feet

Lower-level Entry: 109 square feet

Total Living Area: 2,494 square feet

Width: 60'-0"

Depth: 52'-0"

# EVERYDAY GETAWAY

*A comfy atmosphere prevails from the formal rooms to the wide-open deck.*

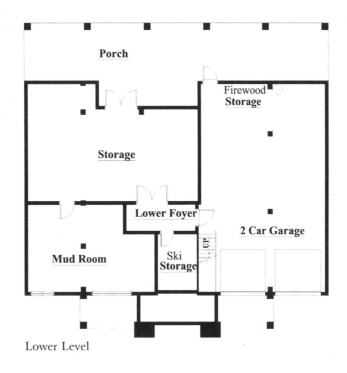

Lower Level

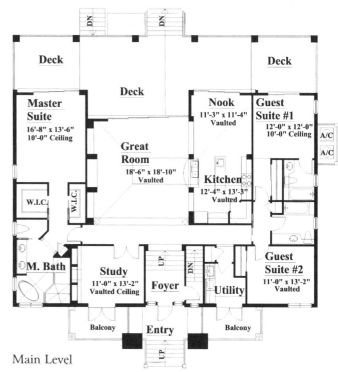

Main Level

Mount Whitney

*Design © The Sater Group*

With a rugged stone-and-siding facade, this neighborhood-friendly home sets the pace in ultra-chic places with timeless character. A stately portico presents a warm welcome, while a mid-level foyer eases the transition to the elevated grand salon. Interior vistas extend throughout the living area, made even more inviting by rows of graceful arches and stunning wide views. A wet bar and pantry serve planned events, and the formal dining room is spacious enough for the most elegant occasions.

In the gourmet kitchen, wide counters and a walk-in pantry surround a food-preparation island that sports a vegetable sink. A pass-through counter permits the cook to participate in conversations in the leisure room. This expansive yet very cozy living space is framed by a mitered wall of glass and warmed by a corner fireplace.

On the other side of the plan, a rambling master suite includes a spacious bath with a whirlpool tub and oversized shower. A private hall leads through a pocket door to a quiet study with built-in cabinetry.

## PLAN HPT030020

Total Living Area: 3,074 square feet
Width: 77'-0"
Depth: 66'-8"

# A Striking Presence

*Never mind the climate, this fresh retreat beats back the weather and brings in the beauty of the outdoors.*

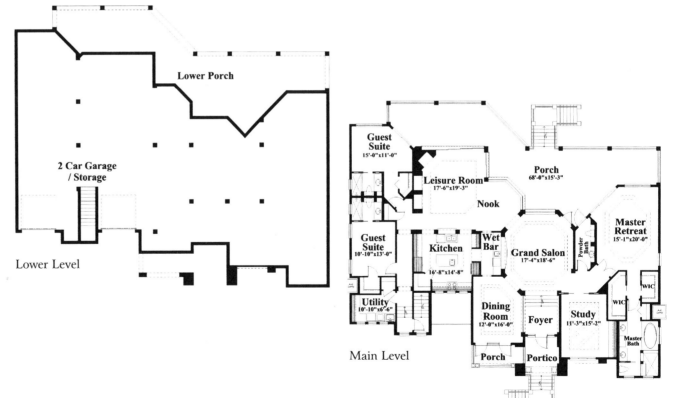

Lower Porch

2 Car Garage / Storage

Lower Level

Guest Suite
15'-0"x11'-0"

Leisure Room
17'-6"x19'-3"

Nook

Porch
68'-0"x15'-3"

Guest Suite
10'-10"x13'-0"

Kitchen
16'-8"x14'-8"

Wet Bar

Grand Salon
17'-4"x18'-6"

Powder Bath

Master Retreat
15'-1"x20'-0"

Utility
10'-10"x6'-6"

Dining Room
12'-0"x16'-0"

Foyer

Study
11'-3"x15'-2"

WIC

WIC

Master Bath

Main Level

Porch

Portico

Eicho Forest

An engaging blend of comfort and high architectural style creates a high-spirited home that's worthy of attention and is downright inviting. The foyer provides a magnificent view through the great room, where a two-story glass wall allows the vista to extend to the rear property. Amenities such as two-sided fireplaces, built-in shelves and cabinetry, wide decks and verandas are perfectly suited to a casual yet elegant lifestyle.

Bedroom 4 shares a fireplace with the great room, while Bedroom 3 provides a beautiful bay window. A gallery hall leads to the living area and formal dining room—a lovely space with mitered walls of sliding glass doors that permit strolls outside. The wraparound veranda includes an outdoor kitchen with a grill, rinsing sink and pass-through to the main kitchen.

The upper-level master suite has its own observation deck and a striking bath with a fireplace, angled whirlpool tub, oversized shower, separate vanities and a walk-in closet with a dressing island. A gallery leads to an elevator and across the catwalk with an overlook to the great room. At the end of the hall, a spacious bedroom offers its own bath and deck, and enough wardrobe space for a live-in guest.

## PLAN HPT030021

Main Level: 2,491 square feet
Upper Level: 1,290 square feet
Lower-level Entry: 358 square feet
Total Living Area: 4,139 square feet
Width: 62'-0"
Depth: 67'-0"

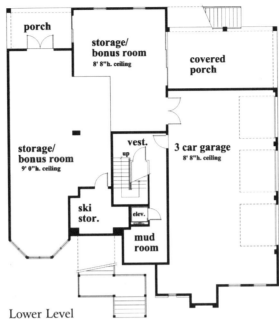

Lower Level

# CASUAL GRANDEUR

*Asymmetrical gables and stately towers combine artful details that borrow freely from the past with innovative verve.*

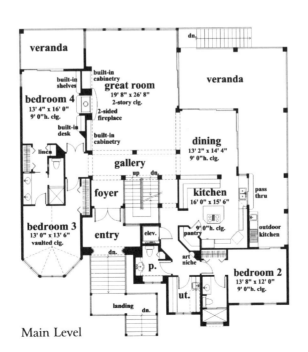

Main Level

Upper Level

SUN-KISSED DECKS

## *joie de vivre*

DREAM ON

COTTAGES

Montego Bay

This beautiful variation of Key West Conch style clearly emphasizes the benefits of living in a sunny clime. An abundance of windows invites warmth and light into this comfortable interior—not to mention invigorating breezes. Teeming with both vertical and horizontal lines, this home will be the darling of the neighborhood. A standing-seam roof mimics a simple balustrade and heritage columns, while louvered shutters echo the classic clapboard siding.

The wraparound porch leads to a descending staircase, which eases the transition from outside to in. The two-story great room boasts a spider-beam ceiling and an entire wall of French doors that open to an entertainment lanai. Graceful arches and decorative columns define an open arrangement of the formal dining room and gourmet kitchen. This well-organized culinary paradise provides a cooktop island with food-preparation space, and a walk-in pantry.

A main-level master suite has its own access to the veranda. Two walk-in closets and a dressing area announce a lavish bath with a magnificent garden tub and a wrapping vanity. On the upper level, each of two guest suites features a walk-in closet and spacious bath.

## PLAN HPT030022

Main Level: 2,096 square feet

Upper Level: 892 square feet

Total Living Area: 2,988 square feet

Width: 58'-0"

Depth: 54'-0"

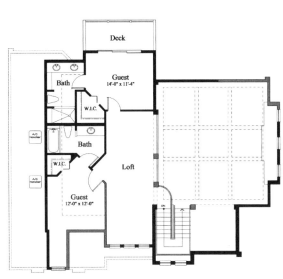

Upper Level

## INNER SPACE

*Open living areas and a grand loft extend the flexibility of this design, with Jamaican louver shutters to let in gentle breezes.*

Main Level

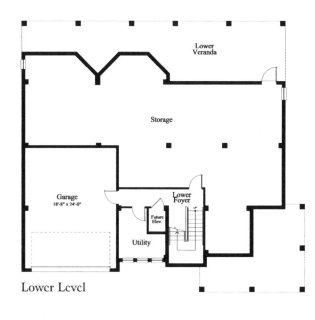

Lower Level

Santa Rosa

This fabulous Key West home blends way-past-cool interior space with the great outdoors. Designed for a balmy climate, this home boasts expansive porches and decks—with outside access from every area of the home. A breath of fresh air, this refined cottage provides a sanctuary of sunlight and moonbeams, with an abundance of windows and glorious French doors and windows.

A sun-dappled foyer leads via a stately mid-level staircase to a splendid great room, which features a warming fireplace tucked in beside beautiful built-in cabinetry. Highlighted by a wall of glass that opens to the rear porch, this two-story living space serves as the stunning heart of the home, and opens to the formal dining room and a well-appointed kitchen.

Spacious secondary bedrooms on the main level open to outside spaces and share a full bath. Upstairs, a ten-foot tray ceiling highlights a very private master suite, which provides French doors to an upper-level porch. The owners bath includes a dual vanity, whirlpool tub, compartmented toilet and oversized shower.

## PLAN HPT030023

Main Level: 1,383 square feet

Upper Level: 595 square feet

Total Living Area: 1,978 square feet

Width: 48'-0"

Depth: 42'-0"

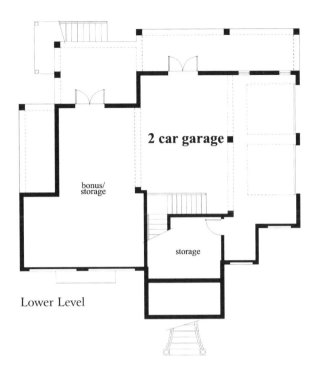

Lower Level

## GREAT GALLERY

*French doors open to decks and covered porches from a savory interior, and a high gallery overlooks the great room.*

Main Level

Upper Level

Linden Place

Design © The Sater Group

This engaging cottage, with an abundance of windows and doors, welcomes the seaside breezes and the gentle winds of cool, moonlit nights. A cozy porch with decorative fretwork and balusters leads through a mid-level entry to the main gallery, which sports an art niche. The great room boasts a warming fireplace, built-in cabinets and two pairs of French doors that open to the rear porch. Large, plentiful windows bathe the formal dining room and spacious living area in sunlight, lending an airy atmosphere and a sense of the outdoors. A detailed kitchen makes preparations easy for the family chef, while the utility room is placed nearby.

In the owners retreat, tall windows and lovely French doors blur the lines between indoors and out. A tray ceiling highlights this private haven. On the upper level, a spacious loft separates two secondary suites that include luxurious amenities. Each of these bedrooms enjoys a tray ceiling, walk-in closet and roomy bath. Two covered porches and an open deck extend the living space with places to enjoy the sights and sounds of the sea.

### PLAN HPT030024

Main Level: 1,510 square feet

Upper Level: 864 square feet

Total Living Area: 2,374 square feet

Bonus Space: 810 square feet

Width: 44'-0"

Depth: 49'-0"

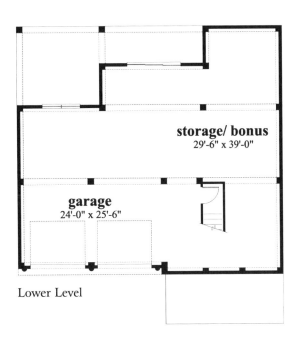

Lower Level

## SWEET TABLEAU

*Graceful arches set off charming windows on this oh-so-perfect facade, rich with simple details.*

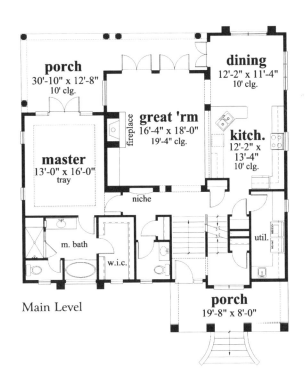

Main Level

Upper Level

Carmel Bay

*Design © The Sater Group*

Arches, columns and French doors pay homage to a captivating Key West style that's light, airy and fully *au courant*. A contemporary, high-pitched hip roof tops a chic compendium of gables, turrets and dormers—the perfect complement to an elegant and breezy entry porch. An open foyer announces a wonderful arrangement of casual space and formal rooms. French doors lead to a quiet study or parlor, which features a wall of built-in shelves and a view of the front property through an arch-topped window. Built-ins frame the fire-place in the great room too, providing an anchor for a wall of glass that brings in a sense of the outdoors.

The main level includes a secluded secondary bedroom, or guest quarters, that's thoughtfully placed near a full bath, coat closet and linen storage. Upstairs, a balcony hall allows interior vistas of the living area below, and connects a secondary bedroom and bath with the master suite. French doors open from both bedrooms to a wrapping deck. The owners bath provides a bumped-out garden tub and a walk-in closet designed for two.

## PLAN HPT030025

Main Level: 1,542 square feet

Upper Level: 971 square feet

Total Living Area: 2,513 square feet

Width: 46'-0"

Depth: 51'-0"

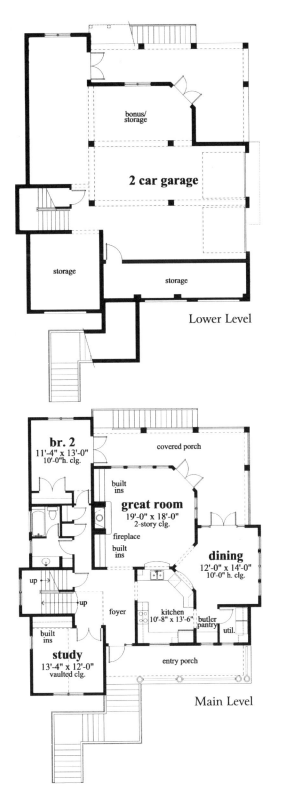

Lower Level

Main Level

# EASY BREEZY

*Comfortable outdoor spaces define this perfect-for-entertaining cottage. Sun-kissed decks and covered porches invite sweet lingering and splendid parties.*

Upper Level

Les Anges

Design © The Sater Group

An inviting wraparound porch and plenty of other outdoor spaces extend the living area of this great cottage. Prevailing summer breezes find their way through 21st-Century rooms, from the foyer to the rear veranda. Built-in cabinetry, a massive fireplace and a host of French doors highlight the central living space, which also features a wet bar.

Nearby, the morning nook provides a bay window and an interior vista that includes the central fireplace. A gourmet kitchen with a food-preparation island serves the formal dining room. Each of the well-defined rooms to the front of the plan sports an elegant ceiling treatment.

The secluded master wing enjoys a bumped-out window, a stunning tray ceiling and twin walk-in closets. Separate vanities and an oversized garden tub grace the owners bath. A private hall leading to the master suite provides a powder room and additional linen storage. The upper level boasts a catwalk that overlooks the great room and the foyer, and connects the two secondary suites. Bedrooms 2 and 3 own walk-in closets, spacious baths and individual access to the upper deck .

## PLAN HPT030026

Main Level: 2,146 square feet

Upper Level: 952 square feet

Lower-level Entry: 187 square feet

Total Living Area: 3,285 square feet

Width: 52'-0"

Depth: 65'-4"

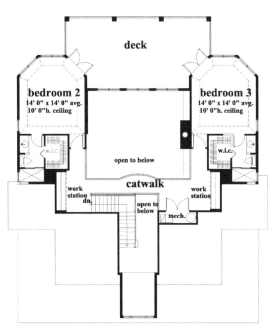

Upper Level

# SINGULAR SENSATION

*Joyful rooms filled with panoramic views and fresh air create a happy environment.*

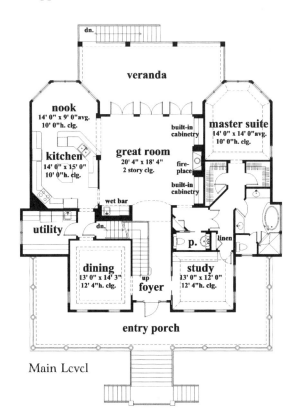

Main Level

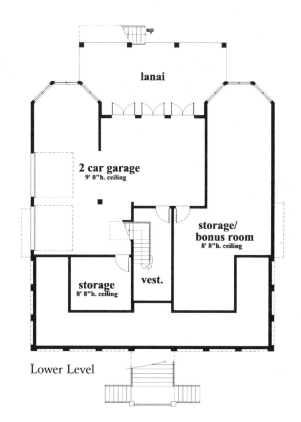

Lower Level

Aruba Bay

*Design © The Sater Group*

Detailed fretwork complements a standing-seam roof on this tropical cottage. An arch-top transom provides an absolutely perfect highlight to the classic clapboard facade. An unrestrained floor plan offers cool digs for kicking back, and a sensational retreat for guests—whether the occasion is formal or casual. French doors open to a rear porch from the great room, letting in fresh air and the sights and sounds of the great outdoors. Triple-window views enhance the formal dining room, which shares its light with the gourmet kitchen.

A genuine retreat, the master suite opens to a private porch, where the fortunate homeowners can gather alone or with the family to talk about the future or simply enjoy the night air. Inside, the owners bedroom leads to a dressing space with linen storage and a walk-in closet. The lavish bath includes a garden tub, oversized shower and a wraparound vanity with two lavatories. Two secondary bedrooms on the upper level share a spacious loft that overlooks the great room. One of the bedrooms opens to a private deck.

## PLAN HPT030027

Main Level: 1,342 square feet

Upper Level: 511 square feet

Total Living Area: 1,853 square feet

Width: 44'-0"

Depth: 40'-0"

Upper Level

## ALL DECKED OUT

*Friendly outdoor spaces invite the best kinds of gatherings on this well-crafted plan, announced by a great front porch.*

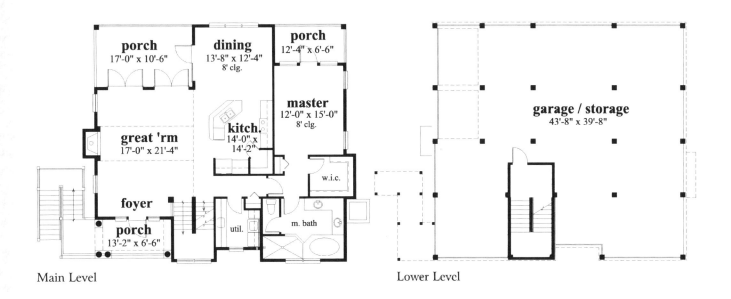

Main Level                    Lower Level

Monterrey Cove

*Design © The Sater Group*

Symmetry is the key to the appeal of this adorable coastal cottage. A standing-seam roof with hipped gables and a charming entry porch with sets of columns create a sense of casual living that is reinforced by the expansive rear veranda. The great room with its glorious views is certainly the centerpiece around which all activities will focus.

A two-story ceiling provides a dramatic upper-level catwalk. Built-ins are partnered with a two-sided fireplace that is shared with the formal dining room. French doors in the great room open to the veranda.

The family chef will find that the island kitchen fulfills their every need. Wrapping counters surround a food-preparation island, and a pass-through counter permits grand views of the outdoors. An archway behind the study leads to the gorgeous master suite. In the owners bedroom, a tray ceiling and bay window add to the sense of spaciousness, while French doors open to the veranda. Each of the upper-level family suites has a walk-in closet and a roomy bath with an oversized shower.

## PLAN HPT030028

Main Level: 1,798 square feet

Upper Level: 900 square feet

Total Living Area: 2,698 square feet

Width: 54'-0"

Depth: 57'-0"

# LAND HANDSOME

*Eyebrow dormers, double columns and a sensational fanlight transom enhance the loveliest surroundings.*

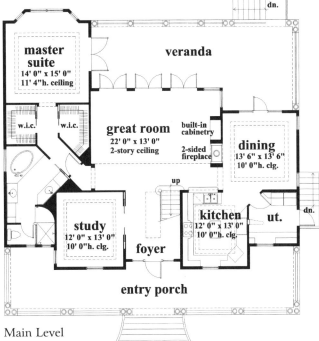

Main Level

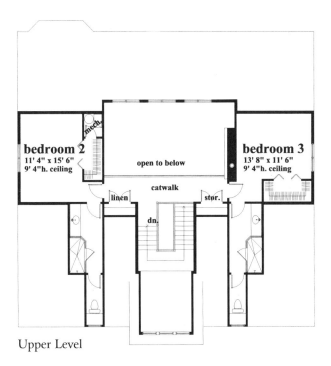

Upper Level

La Palma

Design © The Sater Group

Elements from the Victorian era create this wonderful facade, all decked out with a square tower loft, two-story turret and charming stickwork. A mid-level landing eases the transition from ground level to the entry and foyer. Grand amenities dress the interior with splendor as cottage charm becomes urbane comfort in the living space.

A vaulted ceiling, two-sided fireplace, built-in cabinetry and a wall of glass bring high vogue to an area that's just right for bare feet. Three sets of sliding glass doors open the interior to the wraparound veranda, where the outdoor kitchen provides a pass-through to the gourmet kitchen.

On the main level, Bedroom 4 boasts a private veranda, built-in desk, and a fireplace shared with the great room. To the front of the plan, a spacious guest suite surrounds live-in relatives or extended-stay visitors with a sense of comfort.

A very private secondary suite resides on the upper level with two wardrobes and a private deck. Nearby, a mitered window highlights the owners bedroom, which has its own deck.

## PLAN HPT030029

Main Level: 2,491 square feet

Upper Level: 1,290 square feet

Lower-level Entry: 358 square feet

Total Living Area: 4,139 square feet

Width: 62'-0"

Depth: 67'-0"

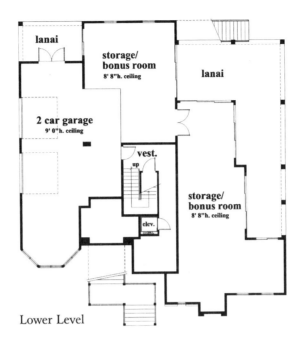

Lower Level

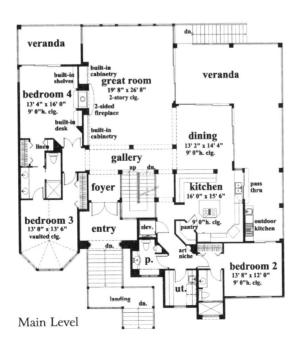

Main Level

## BEAUTIFUL BAYS

*Rows of windows set off a marvelous array of turrets that really bring in the light.*

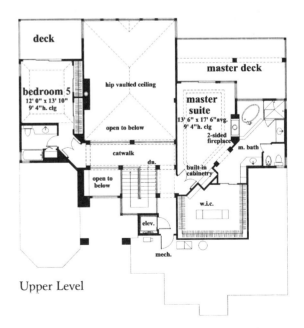

Upper Level

Saint Croix

Design © The Sater Group

Classic columns, beautiful windows and a grand porte cochere set off this dramatic entry. An abundance of windows invite the best views, plenty of sunlight and cool breezes that will open the mind and soothe the spirit. Decorative columns announce the great room, which enjoys a wall of glass and two sets of sliding doors to separate verandas. The well-equipped kitchen serves a morning bay as well as the formal dining room, which provides a servery for planned events.

A secondary suite on the main level offers a sensational bay window. Nearby, a colonnade leads to the study and a quiet space with a window seat. A walk-through cabana bath places the shower by the veranda and stairs, which could lead down to a pool and spa.

A stylish catwalk on the upper level overlooks the great room and foyer and connects guest quarters to the master suite. The highlight of this private haven is a two-sided fireplace that warms both the bedroom and bath. Separate vanities and a walk-in closet designed for two lend a deep sense of luxury.

### PLAN HPT030030

Main Level: 2,391 square feet
Upper Level: 1,539 square feet
Lower-level Entry: 429 square feet
Total Living Area: 4,359 square feet
Width: 71'-0"
Depth: 69'-0"

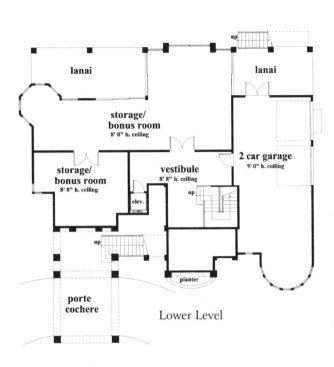

Lower Level

# WARM WELCOME

*This dramatic entry brings a sense of unity to an eclectic theme and complements an inviting porte cochere.*

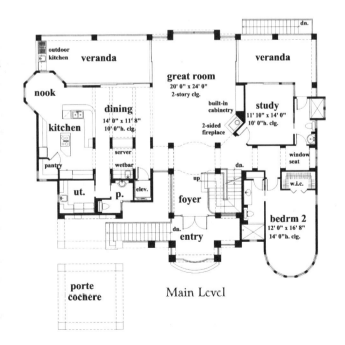

Main Level

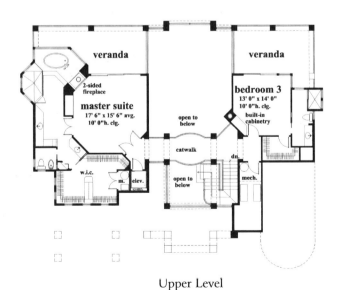

Upper Level

Montserrat

This Southern tidewater cottage is the perfect hideaway—easily blending into the seaside scenery. The Key West style boasts a charming horizontal siding exterior. The wraparound entry porch is relaxing and inviting. Double doors open to the foyer—the study with built-in cabinetry is placed to the right and the formal dining room is to the left.

An octagonal great room with a multi-faceted vaulted ceiling illuminates the interior. This room boasts a fireplace, a built-in entertainment center and three sets of double doors, which lead outside to a vaulted lanai.

The island kitchen is brightened by a bumped-out window and a pass-through to the lanai. Two walk-in closets and a whirlpool bath await to indulge the homeowner in the master suite. A set of double doors opens to the vaulted master lanai for quiet comfort. The U-shaped staircase leads to a loft, which overlooks the great room and the foyer. Upstairs, a computer center and a morning kitchen open to an observation deck.

## PLAN HPT030031

Main Level: 1,855 square feet

Upper Level: 901 square feet

Total Living Area: 2,756 square feet

Width: 66'-0"

Depth: 50'-0"

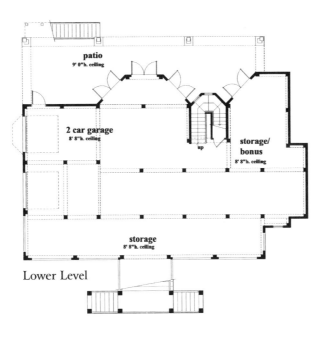

Lower Level

Main Level

## SWEET SYMMETRY

*Dazzling features perfect the curb appeal of this waterside cottage but its real beauty lies within.*

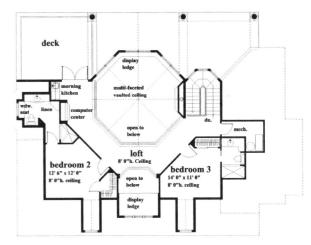

Upper Level

Mimosa

Design © The Sater Group

The individual charm and natural beauty of this sensational home reside in its pure symmetry and perfect blend of past and future. A steeply pitched roof caps an eye-pleasing collection of Prairie-style windows and elegant columns—a mix that feels like home in any region.

The enchanting portico leads to a mid-level foyer, which rises to the grand salon. Wraparound views and open archways answer the call of the great outdoors with a comfortable arrangement of formal rooms that don't feel stuffy. A wide-open leisure room hosts a corner fireplace that's ultra cozy.

The owners wing sprawls from the front portico to the rear covered porch, rich with luxury amenities and plenty of secluded space. A tray ceiling enhances the master bedroom, which opens to a private area of the porch. Two walk-in closets frame a generous dressing space that leads to a sumptuous bath with a garden tub.

On the opposite side of the plan, each of two guest suites has a walk-in closet and private bath. The lower level provides a two-car garage, bonus space and access to a covered porch.

## PLAN HPT030032

Total Living Area: 3,074 square feet

Width: 77'-0"

Depth: 66'-8"

# INDIVIDUAL CHARM

*Oceanfront architecture takes on a new attitude with blissfully simple details and a savory intelligence.*

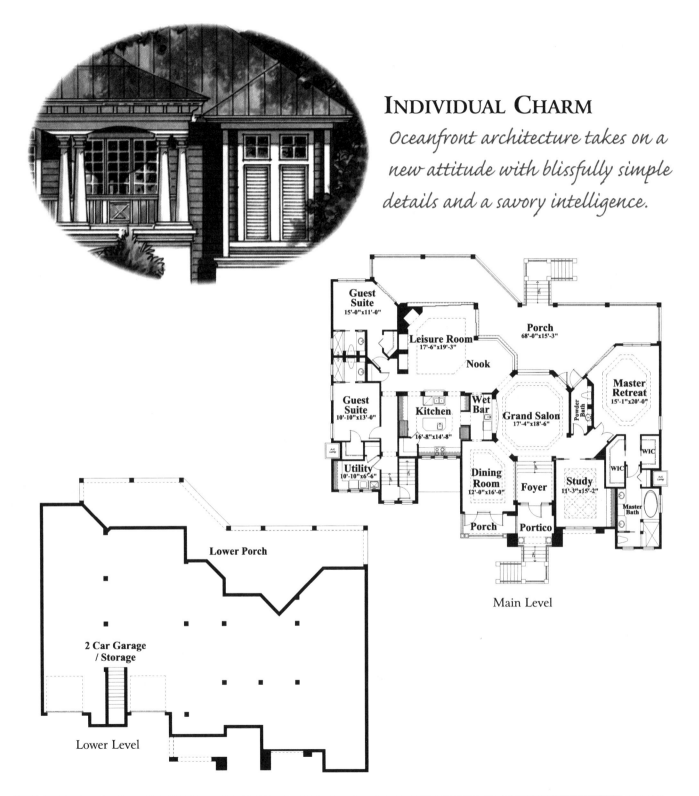

Main Level

Lower Level

Alexandre

This beautiful design is accented by the circular front porch and an abundance of arched windows. The entry leads into a grand foyer, where a radius staircase leads up to secondary sleeping quarters. Most of the rooms in this house are graced with tray, stepped or vaulted ceilings, adding a sense of spaciousness to the plan.

The first-floor master suite boasts many amenities including a private lanai, His and Hers walk-in closets and a bayed tub. Other unique features on the first floor include a study with a window seat and built-in cabinetry, a breakfast nook, a butler's pantry in the island kitchen, a utility room and an outdoor kitchen.

The relaxing leisure room boasts a built-in media center for entertainment and opens through two sets of double doors to the lanai. A two-car garage completes the main floor. The upstairs houses three additional family bedrooms and two full baths. Bedroom 3 boasts an octagonal ceiling, while the ceiling of Bedroom 2 is vaulted. A computer center, linen closet and loft complete the second floor.

## PLAN HPT030033

Main Level: 2,083 square feet

Upper Level: 1,013 square feet

Total Living Area: 3,096 square feet

Width: 74'-0"

Depth: 88'-0"

# PERFECT HARMONY

*Victorian-era architecture and a grand-slam floor plan create a happy union, and a gazebo porch adds fun.*

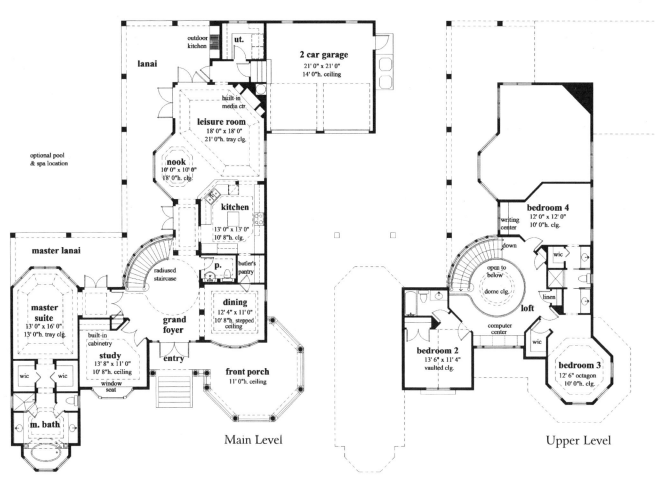

Main Level

Upper Level

Savona Cove

Design © The Sater Group

A magnificent two-story circlehead window takes center stage on this very hip exterior and drenches a three-story staircase with beautiful sunlight. Outside living spaces extend the interior of this sensational Bahamian-style home, bringing the outdoors in with three sets of sliding glass doors. The grand foyer leads to a winding staircase and opens to the great room. An open arrangement of the spacious living area and formal dining room is partially defined by a three-sided fireplace and a wet bar, and the entire space boasts a nine-foot ceiling. The wide veranda is home to an outdoor kitchen. A utility room and two bedrooms, each with a full bath, complete the main level.

The upper level is dedicated to a lavish master suite. A three-sided fireplace warms the master bedroom and a sitting area, which open to an upper deck. Separate baths offer each homeowner a comfortable private retreat: one provides an exercise area and a walk-in shower, while the other boasts a large dressing area. And when it comes to stocking the morning kitchen, the homeowners will appreciate the convenience of the elevator.

## PLAN HPT030034

Main Level: 2,039 square feet

Upper Level: 1,426 square feet

Lower-level Entry: 374 square feet

Total Living Area: 3,839 square feet

Width: 56'-0"

Depth: 54'-0"

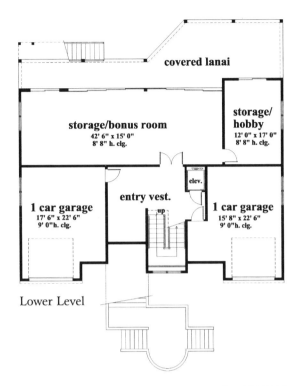

Lower Level

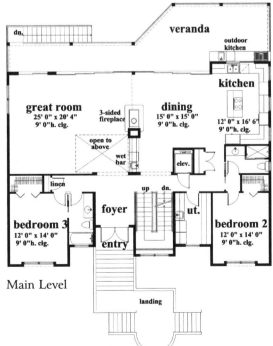

Main Level

## GREAT PERSONALITY

*Arch-top windows take in plenty of sunlight and lend smashing good looks to this fabulous home.*

Upper Level

Papillon

An L-shaped stair rises to a charming entry, lending a sense of Caribbean style to this impressive coastal cottage. Dramatic rooflines cap a host of asymmetrical gables and complement a variety of windows on this visually stunning facade. A mid-level foyer leads up to the main-level great room, which opens to the rear porch through grand French doors, providing views and easing the transition to the outside space.

In the heart of the home, the gourmet kitchen serves a stunning formal dining room with wide views offered through a wall of windows. A guest bath and a convenient laundry are nearby.

To the left of the plan, a secluded master suite boasts a coffered ceiling, walk-in closet and private access to one of the rear porches. The owners bath provides a garden tub, two-sink vanity and linen storage. A grand central staircase leads to the upper-level sleeping quarters and offers a splendid window that brings sunlight indoors. Generous sitting space at the head of the stairs can convert to a computer loft.

## PLAN HPT030035

Main Level: 1,537 square feet

Upper Level: 812 square feet

Total Living Area: 2,349 square feet

Width: 45'-4"

Depth: 50'-0"

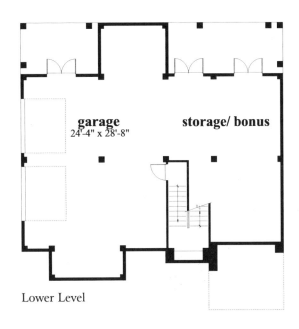

Lower Level

# SIMPLE GEOMETRY

*A French-influenced arched entry mixes past and present, with magnificent gables, tall windows and cool rooflines.*

Main Level

Upper Level

Saint Martin

Cottage accommodations are provided with this seaside vacation dream home. Southern enchantment and Key West style intertwine to create an alluring facade decked in horizontal siding. Once inside, the foyer steps lead up to the formal living areas on the main floor.

To the left, a study is enhanced by a vaulted ceiling and double doors that open onto a front balcony. This room makes a perfect home office for quiet escapes. To the right, a utility room also opens to a front balcony.

Vaulted ceilings create a lofty atmosphere throughout the home, especially in the central great room, which overlooks the rear deck—perfect for summertime entertainment. The island kitchen is open to an adjacent breakfast nook. Guest quarters reside on the right side of the plan—one boasts a private bath.

The master suite is secluded on the left side of the plan for privacy and features two walk-in closets and a pampering whirlpool master bath. Downstairs, storage space abounds alongside the two-car garage.

## AMERICAN HOUSE NOW

*Sensational lines and great symmetry create a great look for tomorrow—ready to build today.*

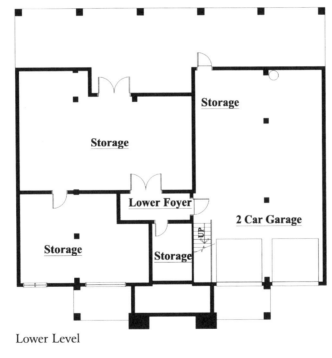

Lower Level

Main Level

### PLAN HPT030036

Main Level: 2,385 square feet
Lower-level Entry: 109 square feet
Total Living Area: 2,494 square feet
Width: 60'-0"
Depth: 52'-0"

Bridgehampton

Exotic tropical breezes will find their way through the joyful rooms of this just-right cottage, bringing with them a sense of tranquility and contentment. Elevated ceilings add a feeling of spaciousness to the wonderfully open design, while the verandas, porch and lanai create lovely outdoor living spaces. The great room, a short flight above the foyer, provides such luxurious amenities as a vaulted ceiling, built-ins, a grand fireplace and an overlook from the upper-level gallery hall.

An efficient island kitchen is nestled between a sunny nook and the formal dining room, which is elegantly defined by regal columns—a perfect place for formal gatherings. Pocket doors open to a private study to the left of the foyer. Secondary sleeping quarters on this level include two family bedrooms that share a full bath, with a laundry conveniently placed nearby.

The upper level is dedicated to the expansive master suite, which boasts a private veranda, tray ceiling, sitting room and walk-in closet. The lower level provides a three-car garage, a lanai and a bonus room for future development.

## PLAN HPT030037

Main Level: 1,671 square feet

Upper Level: 846 square feet

Lower-level Entry: 140 square feet

Total Living Area: 2,657 square feet

Width: 44'-0"

Depth: 55'-0"

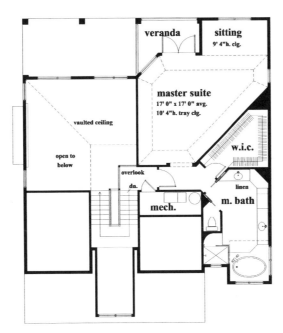

Upper Level

# STUNNING SHOWOFF

*Elements of Southern style mixed with a dash of the future create quite a bit of dazzle and a great floor plan.*

Main Level

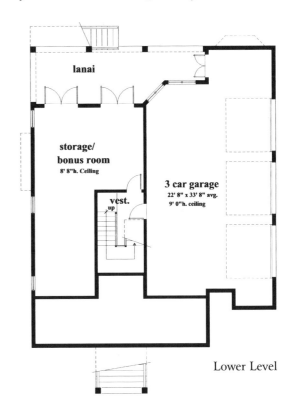

Lower Level

Key Largo

Wraparound porches and a two-story turret give style and charm to this quaint narrow-lot design. The main and upper levels both spill out to outdoor places: a deck upstairs and a veranda below. Built-in cabinetry and a coffered ceiling enhance the great room and lend an elegant touch to an area designed for "shoes are optional" comfort.

A row of French doors opens the formal dining room and the great room to the outside. The well-organized island kitchen resides to the rear of the plan, with a delightfully sunny nook surrounded with windows.

Several windows bathe the upper-level landing and loft with sunshine. Also on this level, a quiet study with a tray ceiling has its own access to the deck. Bedrooms 2 and 3 share a Jack-and-Jill bathroom that boasts a double-sink vanity. And just at the head of the staircase, the luxurious master suite includes a lovely sitting area encircled with a wall of windows. A vaulted ceiling and a cozy two-sided fireplace make this an ideal place to curl up with a novel.

## PLAN HPT030038

Main Level: 1,266 square feet

Upper Level: 1,324 square feet

Total Living Area: 2,590 square feet

Width: 34'-0"

Depth: 63'-2"

# NOVEL IDEA

*Good looks and great planning create this heaven on earth — a just-right place for anywhere.*

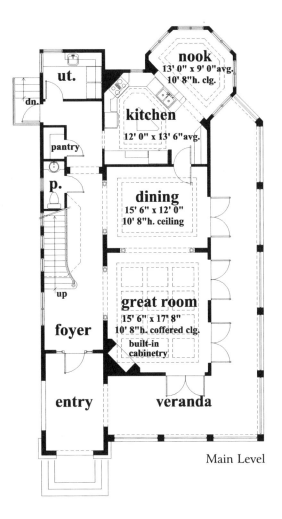

Main Level

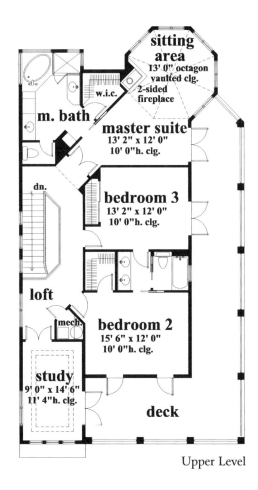

Upper Level

Charleston Hill

With irresistable charm and quiet curb appeal, this enchanting cottage conceals a sophisticated interior that's prepared for busy lifestyles. Of course, dreamy views and French doors flung open to the sounds of the sea surround this modern space, but everyday life needs a place to just be. Try settling into one of two window seats in the main-level great room. Built-in cabinetry frames a massive fireplace, which warms the area and complements the natural views. An open kitchen provides an island with a double sink and snack counter. Planned events are easily served in the formal dining room, but it's a casual space too, with French doors that lead to the veranda.

On the upper level, a central hall with linen storage connects the sleeping quarters. The master suite boasts a walk-in closet and a roomy bath with a dual-sink vanity. A compartmented bath and an oversized shower complete this relaxing retreat. Each of two secondary bedrooms has plenty of wardrobe space. Bedroom 3 leads out to the upper-level deck. The main staircase also leads to the lower-level entry porch, a rear lanai and a two-car garage that permits a smaller third vehicle.

## PLAN HPT030039

Main Level: 874 square feet

Upper Level: 880 square feet

Lower-level Entry: 242 square feet

Total Living Area: 1,996 square feet

Width: 34'-0"

Depth: 43'-0"

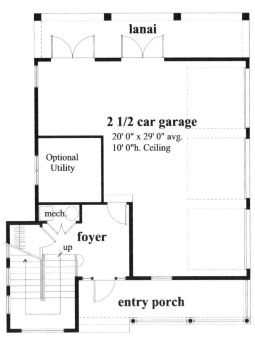

Lower Level

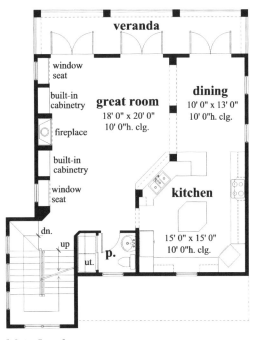

Main Level

# SOUTHERN ACCENTS

*Refined details that call up the past mix it up with a New World beauty that's all the rage.*

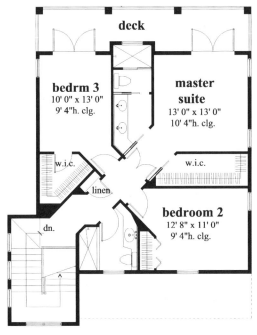

Upper Level

Laguna Beach

Design © The Sater Group

Stunning arch-top windows place this spacious cottage at the top of its class. So much more than just a pretty face, this home is packed with personality—not to mention great views. From the entry to the rear balcony, vistas abound through walls of glass that line the rear of the plan, permitting outside and inside to mingle. A formal dining room opens through a colonnade from the central gallery hall and shares the comfort of the fireplace in the great room.

A food-preparation island and cooktop peninsula highlight a well-planned kitchen, which provides a walk-in pantry. Serving formal events is easy, with a open arrangement that allows guests to enjoy the veranda and balcony.

One of the best features of the house is the master suite, with views and access to a private porch. Two walk-in closets frame a private dressing space and lead to a spacious angled bath with a garden tub. On the opposite side of the plan, each of two guest suites features a roomy bath. Suite 2 leads out to the veranda.

## PLAN HPT030040

Total Living Area: 2,430 square feet

Width: 70'-2"

Depth: 53'-0"

# MODERN PERFECT

*Formal rooms take on casual lifestyles with a shoes-are-optional attitude and nothing but style outside.*

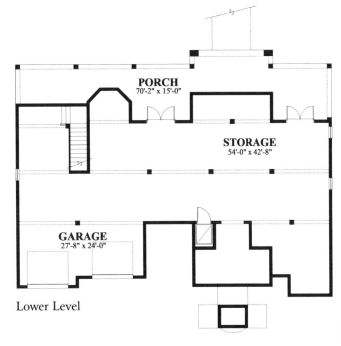

Lower Level

Main Level

Newport Cove

Design © The Sater Group

The Sater Design Collection

This raised Tidewater design is well suited for many building situations, with comfortable outdoor areas that encourage year-round living. Horizontal siding and a steeply pitched roof call up a sense of the past, while a smart-space interior redefines the luxury of comfort with up-to-the-minute amenities. A hip vaulted ceiling highlights the great room, made comfy by a centered fireplace, extensive built-ins and French doors that let in fresh air and sunlight. Fling the doors open for any occasion and mix outdoors with in.

The formal dining room opens from the entry hall and features a triple-window view of the side property. Guests may wish to kick off their shoes and linger outside under the stars on the pretty front porch. Family members will gather in the morning nook or at the snack counter in the kitchen.

Sunlight fills this great house, but quiet space is easy to find too. A secluded sitting area in the master suite features a wide window and a door to a private area of the rear porch. Each of two secondary bedrooms has a triple window and an ample wardrobe.

## PLAN HPT030041

Total Living Area: 2,136 square feet

Width: 44'-0"

Depth: 63'-0"

# GIMME SHELTER

*A deep overhang shelters the entry porch yet sunlight gladly streams in through glorious windows.*

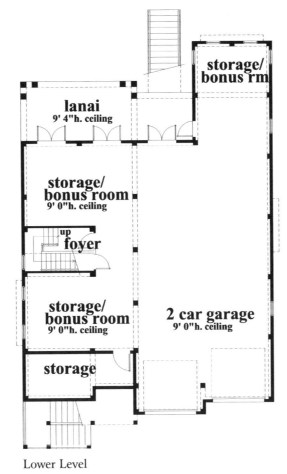

Lower Level

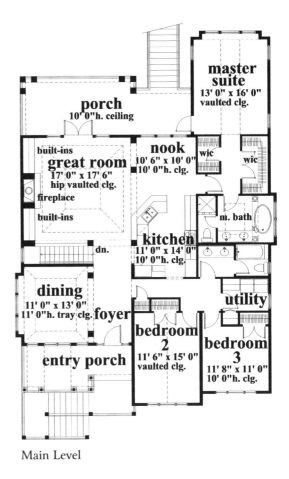

Main Level

Plymouth Bay

This quaint Southern cottage boasts seaside elegance—perfect for a vacation retreat. Horizontal siding and unique window accents lend a slight gothic grace to the exterior facade. The entry leads to the foyer and to the two-story great room, which illuminates the spacious interior. This room provides a warming fireplace and offers built-in cabinetry. Double doors open onto an enticing veranda, which wraps around to the rear deck.

The dining room also extends through double doors to the veranda on the left side on the plan. The kitchen offers an efficient pantry. An additional bedroom and a private bath, a powder room and a utility room also reside on this floor.

Upstairs, a vaulted ceiling enhances the master suite and private bath. A private deck from the owners retreat can be accessed through a set of double doors. The loft area, which overlooks the great room, accesses a second deck. The basement-level bonus room and storage area share space with a two-car garage. Two lanais open on either side of the bonus room for additional patio space.

## PLAN HPT030042

Main Level: 1,143 square feet

Upper Level: 651 square feet

Total Living Area: 1,794 square feet

Width: 32'-0"

Depth: 57'-0"

# TURN OF THE CENTURY

*Pristine lines and Gothic details radiate soul in a smart town-house that rocks with beauty.*

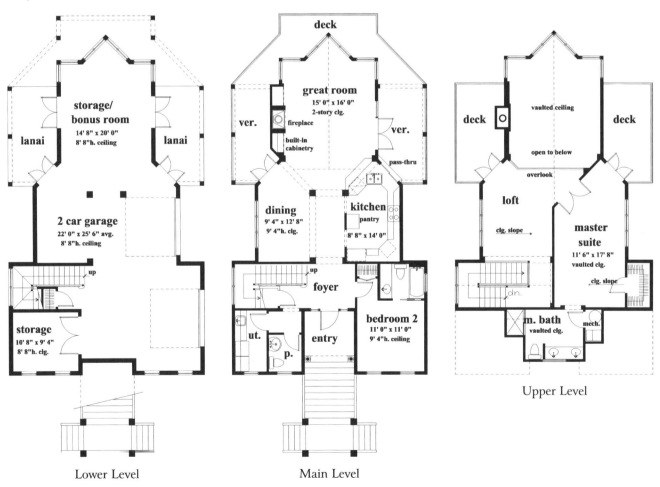

Lower Level

Main Level

Upper Level

VIEWS

OPEN-AIR VIEWS

# gentle breezes

LIVE A LITTLE

*live a little*

94

VILLAS

*Design © The Sater Group*

*Mission Hills*

This enticing European villa boasts an Italian charm and a distinctly Mediterranean feel. Stucco and columns dramatically enhance the stately facade. Inside, the foyer steps lead up to the formal living areas. To the left, a study is expanded by a vaulted ceiling and double doors that open to the front balcony. This room makes a perfect library or parlor, and easily converts to a home office.

To the right of the plan, an efficient laundry sports a private balcony. Vaulted ceilings create a sense of spaciousness throughout the home, and enhance the interior vistas provided by the central great room, which overlooks the rear deck. The island kitchen is conveniently open to a breakfast nook. The guest quarters reside on the right side of the plan—one boasts a private bath, while the second suite uses a full hall bath.

The master suite is secluded to the left for privacy, and features two walk-in closets, a dual-sink vanity and whirlpool tub. Sliding glass doors open the homeowner's retreat to a private area of the rear deck. Downstairs, the two-car garage provides additional storage space.

## PLAN HPT030043

Main Level: 2,385 square feet

Lower-level Entry: 109 square feet

Total Living Area: 2,494 square feet

Width: 60'-0"

Depth: 52'-0"

# WORLD CLASS

*Be bold. Define a very personal beauty that's cutting edge yet entirely suited for a no-shoes lifestyle.*

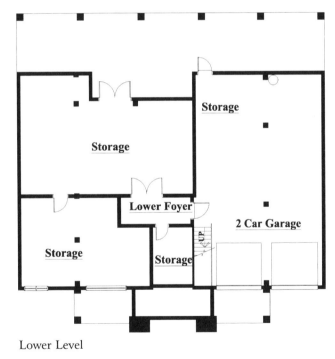

Lower Level

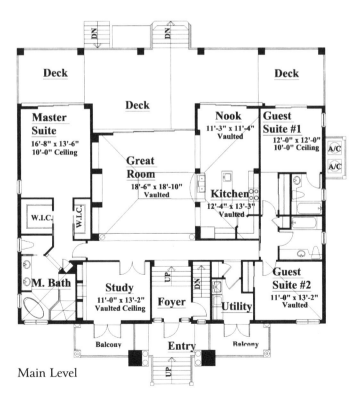

Main Level

*Design © The Sater Group*

Jupiter Bay

Light, views and open interior spaces expand the feel and flow of this European cottage home. A vaulted entry leads down a sheltered staircase to the stunning porte cochere—an enhancement that's as practical as it is beautiful. This livable home design maximizes the appreciation of its views with wide verandas and covered lanais.

Secluded to the rear of the main level, a study provides private access to a cabana bath that leads to the veranda and rear property, which may include a pool or spa, or even a path to the ocean. The formal dining room is served by a gourmet kitchen, butler's pantry and wet bar, and features its own access to the outdoors.

An elevator near the foyer and central stairs leads to the upper and lower levels. Upstairs, a catwalk allows overlooks to the great room and foyer, and connects the master suite with a secondary bedroom or guest suite. Each suite leads to a private veranda—a wonderful place to take advantage of breezes and views.

## PLAN HPT030044

Main Level: 2,391 square feet

Upper Level: 1,539 square feet

Lower-level Entry: 429 square feet

Total Living Area: 4,359 square feet

Width: 71'-0"

Depth: 69'-0"

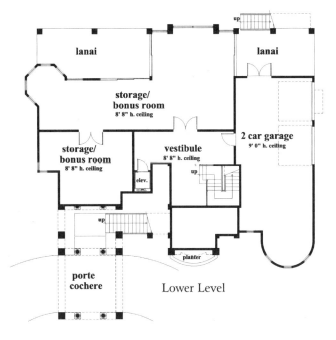

Lower Level

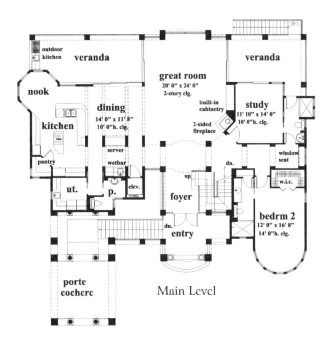

Main Level

# WONDROUS VIEWS

*Tall windows and transoms line a dazzling bay turret and lend a sense of romance and charm—not to mention the views.*

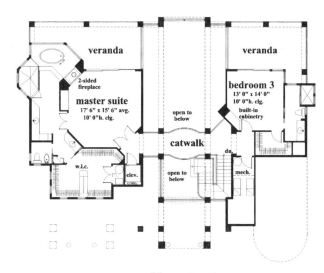

Upper Level

Hyatt Park

Chic and glamorous, this Mediterranean facade pairs ancient shapes, such as square columns, with a refined disposition set off by radius windows. A magnificent entry leads to an interior gallery and great room. This extraordinary space is warmed by a two-sided fireplace and defined by extended views of the rear property. Sliding glass doors to a wraparound veranda create great indoor/outdoor flow.

The gourmet kitchen easily serves any occasion and provides a pass-through to the outdoor kitchen. The front of the plan also includes a guest suite, which features an oversized shower and ample wardrobe space. Nearby, a powder room accommodates visitors, while an elevator leads to the sleeping quarters upstairs.

Double doors open to the master suite, which features a walk-in closet, two-sided fireplace and angled whirlpool bath. The owners bedroom boasts a tray ceiling and doors to a spacious deck—a private retreat where a homeowner can find repose. The upper-level catwalk leads to a bedroom suite that can easily accommodate a guest or live-in relative.

## PLAN HPT030045

Main Level: 2,491 square feet

Upper Level: 1,290 square feet

Lower-level Entry: 358 square feet

Total Living Area: 4,139 square feet

Width: 62'-0"

Depth: 67'-0"

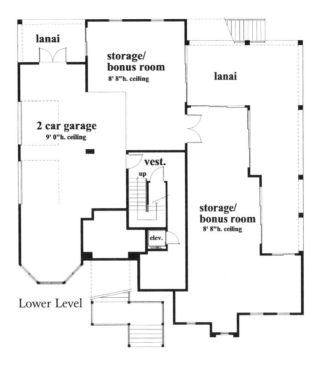

Lower Level

# GENTLE EUROPEAN

*Finely detailed flourishes deck out this easygoing elevation, front to back, with a basic sense of the past.*

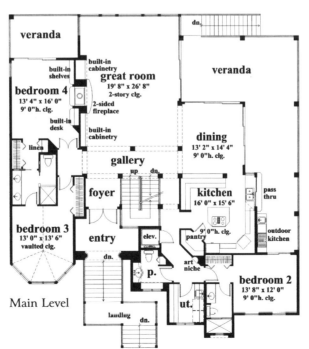

Main Level

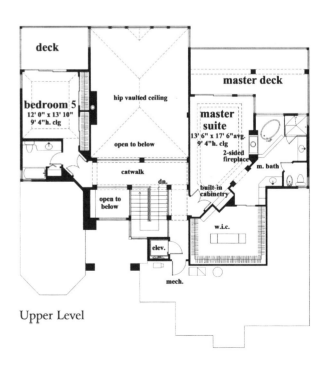

Upper Level

San Marino

Design © The Sater Group

With a row of pretty windows, this gentle Mediterranean home offers plenty of views and outdoor spaces for mingling with nature. A sunburst transom creates a gorgeous entry that will be the envy of the neighborhood. Pilasters announce a grand sense of the past and offer a warm welcome to an ultra-plush interior. These inner vistas, plus the outdoor views, mix it up with fresh air and breezes stirring from open doors to the veranda. High ceilings in the great room and dining room extend the sense of spaciousness and propose planned events that spill out to the outdoor spaces.

From the entry to the rear balcony, panoramas abound through walls of glass that line the rear of the plan. The formal dining room opens through a colonnade from the central gallery hall and shares the comfort of the central fireplace. A food-preparation island and service counter allow easy meals or fabulous dinners.

Of course, the best part of the eating area is the morning nook—a bright reprieve surrounded with the beauty of sunshine and trees. Never mind the weather: seize the morning with pancakes and syrup. Guests may wish to linger on the rear balcony, which provides steps down to a lower-level porch.

## PLAN HPT030046

Total Living Area: 2,433 square feet
Width: 70'-2"
Depth: 53'-0"

# HIP CHATEAU

*In a plan designed for the future, elegant details find a home in a place that allows the outdoors in to mingle with open spaces.*

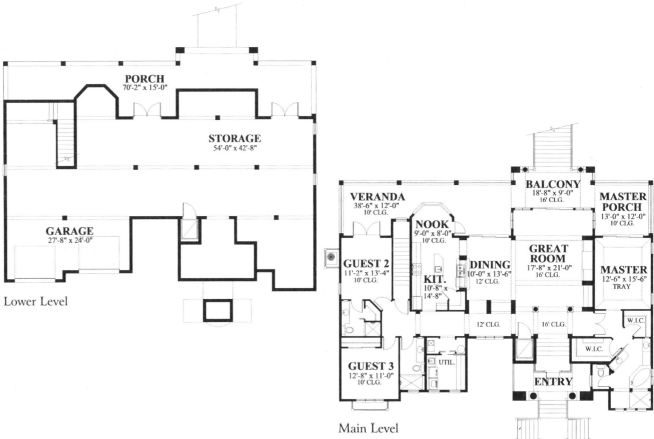

Lower Level

Main Level

Royal Marco

Design © The Sater Group

Villa enchantment is romantically enhanced by the facade of this Italianate design—Mediterranean allure creates the soft European appeal. The wraparound entry porch is inviting. Enter through double doors to the two-story foyer—notice the study with built-in cabinetry to the right and the formal dining room to the left. Straight ahead, an octagonal great room with a multi-faceted vaulted ceiling illuminates the entire plan. This room offers a fireplace, a built-in entertainment center and three sets of double doors, which lead outside to a vaulted lanai. The island kitchen is brightened by a bayed window and a pass-through to the lanai.

Two spacious walk-in closets and a whirlpool bath pamper the homeowner in the master suite. A set of double doors opens to the vaulted master lanai for relaxing comfort. A U-shaped staircase winds upstairs to a loft, which overlooks the great room and the foyer. Two additional family bedrooms each feature private baths. A computer center and a morning kitchen at the end of the hallway open to the outer deck.

## PLAN HPT030047

Main Level: 1,855 square feet

Upper Level: 901 square feet

Total Living Area: 2,756 square feet

Width: 66'-0"

Depth: 50'-0"

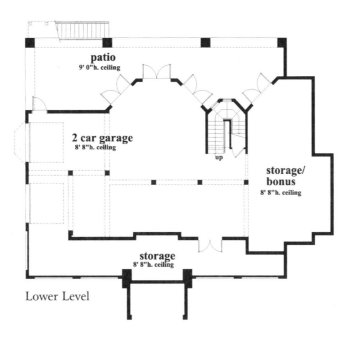

Lower Level

# HOUSE BEAUTIFUL

*An arch-top transom and massive pediment bring a sweet familiarity to a fresh face.*

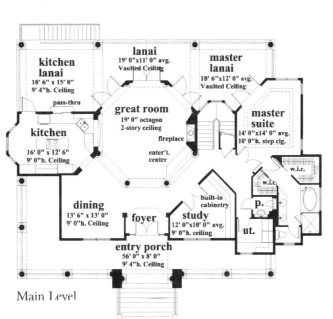

Main Level

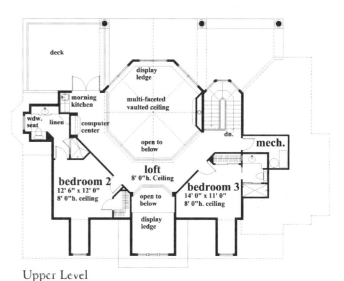

Upper Level

*Casa Bella*

Historic architectural details and time-less materials come together in this outrageously beautiful home. With a perfect Mediterranean spirit, arch-top windows create curb appeal and allow the beauty and warmth of nature within. An unrestrained interior blends formal and casual living spaces, with exceptional touches such as a row of French doors and lovely windows. To the rear of the plan, an elegant dining room easily flexes to serve traditional events as well as impromptu gatherings. An angled island counter accents the gourmet kitchen and permits wide interior vistas.

The homeowner's retreat features a spacious bedroom that leads outside to a private porch—the best place in the world to count stars. Lovely windows really let in the light, creating a true respite from the honks and beeps of city life. An area framed by the walk-in closet and linen storage leads to a lavish bath with a garden tub and oversized shower. On the upper level, an open deck extends the square footage of one of the secondary bedrooms—an invitation to enjoy sunlight and gentle breezes.

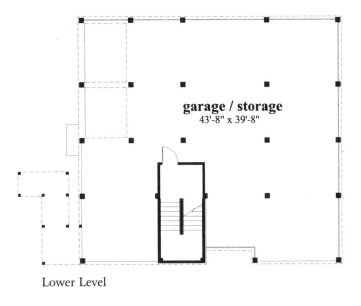

garage / storage
43'-8" x 39'-8"

Lower Level

# HEART OF GOLD

*An arch-top transom announces a glorious interior that's ready for any event and comfortable enough for bare feet.*

## PLAN HPT030048

Main Level: 1,342 square feet

Upper Level: 511 square feet

Total Living Area: 1,853 square feet

Width: 44'-0"

Depth: 40'-0"

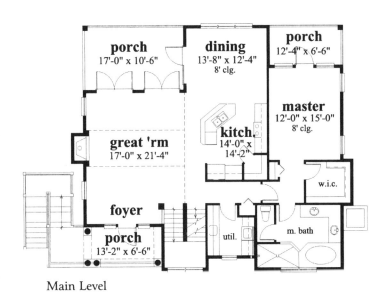

porch
17'-0" x 10'-6"

dining
13'-8" x 12'-4"
8' clg.

porch
12'-4" x 6'-6"

master
12'-0" x 15'-0"
8' clg.

great 'rm
17'-0" x 21'-4"

kitch.
14'-0" x
14'-2"

w.i.c.

foyer

util.

m. bath

porch
13'-2" x 6'-6"

Main Level

open deck
17'-0" x 10'-6"

bedroom
13'-8" x 12'-0"
12' clg.

open

loft

bath

bedroom
10'-0" x 13'-2"
12' clg.

Upper Level

*Sunset Beach*

The Sater Design Collection

This country villa is accented by a gazebo-style front porch and an abundance of arched windows. The entry leads into the grand foyer, where a sweeping radius staircase impresses. Most of the rooms in this house are graced with tray, stepped or vaulted ceilings, enhancing the entire plan.

The main-level master suite boasts multiple amenities, including a private lanai, two walk-in closets and a bayed whirlpool tub. Other highlights on this floor include a study with a window seat and built-in cabinetry, a bayed breakfast nook, a convenient butler's pantry in the island kitchen, a utility room and an outdoor kitchen on the lanai.

The enticing leisure room boasts a built-in media center for home entertainment and opens through two sets of double doors to the lanai. A two-car garage completes the main floor. Three secondary bedrooms reside upstairs, along with two full baths. Bedroom 3 offers an octagonal ceiling, while Bedroom 2 features a vaulted ceiling. A computer center, linen area and a loft overlooking the grand foyer complete the second floor.

## JUST BEAUTIFUL

*Renaissance proportions make the rooms of this grand manor feel generous and serene.*

### PLAN HPT030049

Main Level: 2,083 square feet

Upper Level: 1,013 square feet

Total Living Area: 3,096 square feet

Width: 74'-0"

Depth: 88'-0"

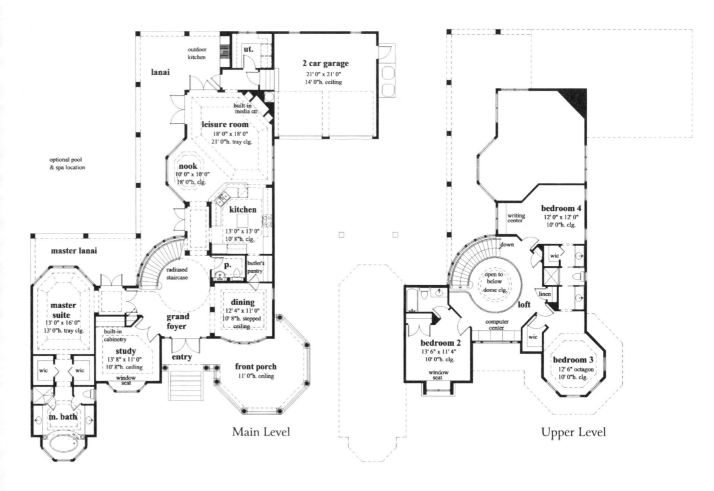

Main Level

Upper Level

Villa Tucano

The Sater Design Collection

A stunning transom creates a picture-perfect entry and a glorious complement to the arch-top windows with this exquisite villa. Double stairs embraced by a classic balustrade lead to a mid-level landing, easing the transition from ground level to the front door. The foyer opens to a central gallery, which enjoys extensive views through the interior. Amenities in the great room create an inviting environment for crowd-size entertaining or cozy gatherings. A balcony overlook provides an elegant touch, while a wet bar and three-sided fireplace help define the space and add comfort and convenience.

The formal dining room opens to a gourmet kitchen, which provides lots of counter space, a cooktop island and a pass-through to the outdoor kitchen. Nearby, a secondary bedroom adjoins a full bath and can be converted to guest quarters.

The upper level is dedicated to the spacious master retreat, packed with luxury amenities. Separate baths include an exercise room and walk-in shower, and linen storage, dressing space and a double walk-in closet. Separate garages on the lower level lead to an entry vestibule with both an elevator and stairs.

## PLAN HPT030050

Main Level: 2,039 square feet

Upper Level: 1,426 square feet

Lower-level Entry: 374 square feet

Total Living Area: 3,839 square feet

Width: 56'-0"

Depth: 54'-0"

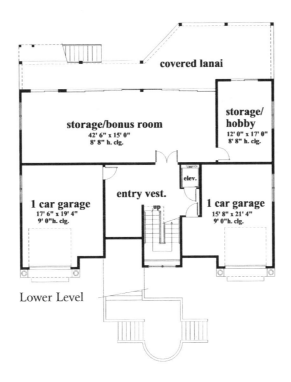

Lower Level

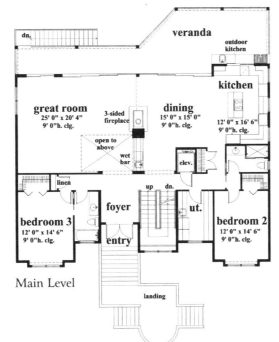

Main Level

## OPEN HOUSE

*An engaging blend of old and new, this European villa speaks of gentler times with a new-century attitude and a smart interior.*

Upper Level

*Château-sur-Mer*

A romantic air flirts with the clean simple lines of this Mediterranean villa. Hip roofs and varied gables call up a past rich with history but also speak of a style that's nearly futuristic. Classic curves announce the covered entry porch, which provides wraparound views and a breezy place to lose the shoes. An enchanting mix of Doric columns and sleek fasciae set off a shapely balustrade and exalt an array of arch-top windows, creating a vibrant facade that's both timeless and trendy.

Open and sophisticated, its broad interior is made cozy by a refined arrangement of rooms that's thoroughly modern and downright comfortable. Arches deck the passageways to the two-story great room, and three sets of French doors invite natural light and a *bon vivant* spirit to fill this comfortable gathering space.

A spider-beam ceiling, built-in bookshelves and a fireplace define the room, while a sprawling lanai blurs the line between outdoors and in—a perfect arrangement for traditional events and intimate gatherings. In the main-level master suite, a wall of glass allows panoramic views and permits access to the lanai. Upstairs, a computer loft offers a balcony overlook.

## CHIC AND SIMPLE

*Savory comfort hugs the tantalizing blend of dreamy windows and clean lines that set off this stunning interpretation of Mediterranean style.*

### PLAN HPT030051

Main Level: 2,096 square feet

Upper Level: 892 square feet

Total Living Area: 2,988 square feet

Width: 56'-0"

Depth: 54'-0"

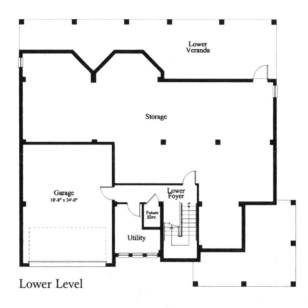

Lower Level

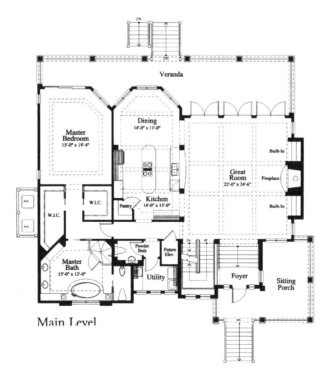

Main Level

Upper Level

Nicholas Park

Design © The Sater Group

With graceful arches and rows of beautiful windows, this chic villa plans for the future with an upper-level loft suitable for surfing the web. Sleeping quarters on this level define luxury with separate access to an open deck and private porches. The entry porch provides a mid-level landing that rises to the living space. Here, plenty of windows and open French doors lend light and a sense of spaciousness to the great room, which features a fireplace.

An art niche decks out a private area of the gallery hall leading to the master suite, and French doors open the master bedroom to the rear porch. A tray ceiling highlights the suite, which boasts a roomy bath with a garden tub. A U-shaped walk-in closet permits a dressing area, while an oversized shower and nearby vanity offer a convenient arrangement for the bath. Just off the foyer, a powder room maintains privacy for the master wing. The lower level provides bonus space, additional storage and a two-car garage.

### PLAN HPT030052

Main Level: 1,510 square feet

Upper Level: 864 square feet

Total Living Area: 2,374 square feet

Width: 44'-0"

Depth: 48'-0"

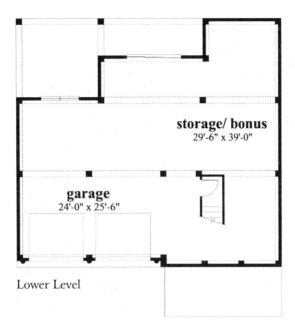

Lower Level

## GREAT VISION

*Rows of sunburst transoms set off this brave, exquisite facade, while bold columns create a grand entry.*

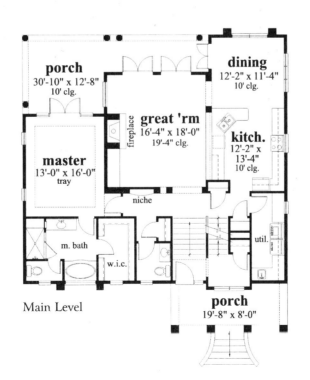

Main Level

Upper Level

Riviera dei Fiori

Design © The Sater Group

The Sater Design Collection

Stately and elegant, this home displays fine Tuscan columns, fanlight windows, hipped gables and a detailed balustrade that splash its facade with a subtle European flavor. Inside, a dramatic winding staircase provides a focal point to the grand entry. The foyer opens to the true heart of this home, the two-story great room.

With imaginative angles and a multitude of windows and French doors, the great room holds a magnificent fireplace nestled with built-in cabinetry. A secluded study to the left of the foyer is perfectly suited for quiet moments of reflection and intimate entertaining.

The formal dining room boasts a fabulous view of the outdoors as well as access to the expansive covered porch via French doors. A butler's pantry eases the service of the well-equipped kitchen, with a conveniently placed utility room nearby.

A second-floor gallery hall provides an overlook to the great room. The private master suite boasts a dual-sink vanity, compartmented toilet, separate shower, garden tub and walk-in closet. The sitting area allows marvelous views and provides French doors to the deck.

## PLAN HPT030053

Main Level: 1,542 square feet

Upper Level: 971 square feet

Total Living Area: 2,513 square feet

Width: 46'-0"

Depth: 51'-0"

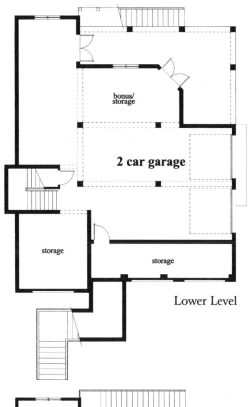

Lower Level

Main Level

## SERENITY NOW

*sun-splashed and fun, this sweet manor boasts a wealth of dreamy windows and very comfortable rooms.*

Upper Level

Chelsea Passage

Great indoor/outdoor living is accomplished in this home through glass doors that offer easy access to rear porches, which provide perfect areas to entertain. From a dramatic mid-level entry with a colonnaded stairway, a gallery opens to the great room, where two sets of French doors bring in the beauty and warmth of natural light.

An air of comfortable elegance prevails throughout this spacious home. The gourmet kitchen boasts an interior vista that includes the great room's fireplace. The formal dining room features a wall of glass, which furthers the spacious feeling of the interior and allows outdoor views that are simply dazzling.

Splendid amenities abound in the master suite, where a dressing area and walk-in closet lead to a spacious and well-organized bath. A garden tub and separate shower reside near a vanity and additional linen storage. The master bedroom provides access to a private porch through stylish French doors.

## PLAN HPT030054

Main Level: 1,537 square feet

Upper Level: 812 square feet

Total Living Area: 2,349 square feet

Width: 45'-4"

Depth: 50'-0"

Lower Level

## GRAND OPENING

*A well-crafted entry with a radius window and glass panels offers a warm welcome and more than just a bit of dazzle.*

Main Level

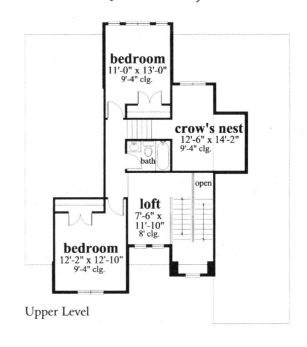

Upper Level

Villa Caprini

A stately tower adds a sense of grandeur to cool, contemporary high-pitched rooflines on this dreamy Mediterranean-style villa. Old World details such as corner quoins, a faux widow's walk and gentle arches, lend definition and dignity to the facade, while well-planned rooms and wide-open spaces reside within. Surrounded by outdoor views, the living space extends to a veranda through three sets of French doors. Decorative columns announce the dining area, which boasts a ten-foot ceiling and views of its own. Cozy gatherings and casual events will fit nicely in this perfect place, easily served by a gourmet kitchen.

Tall arch-top windows bathe a winding staircase with sunlight or moonlight, and permit the homeowner to enjoy vacation views as a part of everyday life. The upper-level sleeping quarters include a homeowner's retreat that offers a high-vogue bedroom with views and access to the observation deck. The master bedroom provides a tray ceiling, and an oversized shower highlights the bath. Secondary bedrooms share a full bath and linen storage. Bedroom 3 features a walk-in closet and French doors to the deck.

## PLAN HPT030055

Main Level: 874 square feet

Upper Level: 880 square feet

Lower-level Entry: 242 square feet

Total Living Area: 1,996 square feet

Width: 34'-0"

Depth: 43'-0"

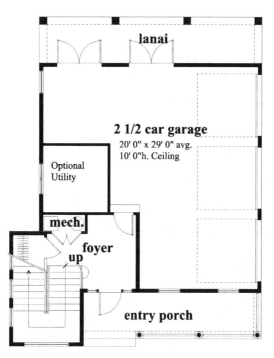

Lower Level

Main Level

# TURNING HEADS

*Dazzlingly beautiful details make this one of the best Sun Country designs for everyday living or a winter getaway.*

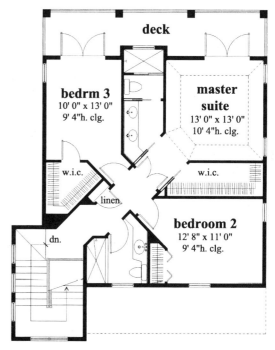

Upper Level

Coconut Grove

Design © The Sater Group

Architectural details that were popular during the nineteenth century have been translated into a modern vernacular with this stunning Southern design. Simple balustrades and broad arches frame a glass-paneled entry that's further enhanced by a turret. A vaulted foyer leads upstairs and to a spacious main-level great room.

Charming details in the casual living space include a wet bar, fireplace and three sets of French doors that lead to an entertainment veranda. While the interior space provides the feel of a contemporary home, an eclectic mix of accoutrements—from carved niches to coffered ceilings—reflects vernacular styles of Southern regions.

A bay window brightens the master suite and provides views of the veranda and rear property. Two walk-in closets frame a spacious dressing area and announce a lavish bath with separate vanities and a garden tub. A hall that offers linen storage leads to a quiet study, which also opens from the foyer.

## PLAN HPT030056

Main Level: 2,146 square feet

Upper Level: 952 square feet

Lower-level Entry: 187 square feet

Total Living Area: 3,285 square feet

Width: 52'-0"

Depth: 65'-4"

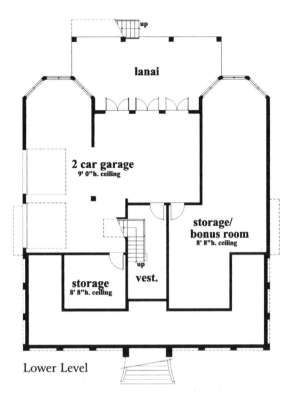

Lower Level

Main Level

## PICTURE PERFECT

*A keystone accent tops an elegant presentation of simple architectural details that call up the past.*

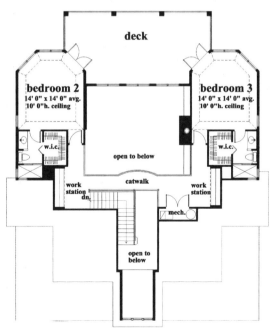

Upper Level

Biscayne Bay

The Sater Design Collection

A seamless fusion of cosmopolitan elan and shoes-off nonchalance, this tropical villa is a happy compromise of high vogue and deep comfort. Old World window treatments contribute to a blend of traditional and contemporary elements outside. Soaring interior vistas and bountiful outdoor views create a sense of ease and comfort within.

The study makes a statement of allegiance to historic sensibilities, with a tray ceiling, crown moldings and a muntin window. French doors, built-in cabinetry and a through-fireplace create a rich ambiance in the two-story great room. A few steps from the gourmet kitchen, the formal dining room invites crowd-size gatherings that spill onto the veranda.

The master suite has a bumped-out bay window and stunning French doors that lead outside. Walk-in closets frame the dressing area and announce a well-accoutered bath, which boasts a garden tub and separate shower. Upstairs, two bedroom suites share a catwalk that offers a spectacular view extending beyond the great room to the outdoors. Each suite provides a spacious dormer-style bath.

## PLAN HPT030057

Main Level: 1,798 square feet

Upper Level: 900 square feet

Total Living Area: 2,698 square feet

Width: 54'-0"

Depth: 57'-0"

# PRIVATE PARADISE

*Live well and prosper in a golden oceanfront home that's hip and out-of-this-world beautiful.*

Main Level

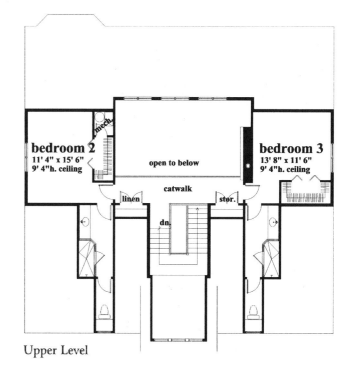

Upper Level

Barcelona Harbor

Design © The Sater Group

This stunning paradise achieves its casual European character by mixing Spanish and French influences. A fanlight transom caps the stately entry and speaks volumes about timeless beauty. The dazzling portico leads to a mid-level foyer and to the grand salon—a magnificent room of graceful arches and endless views.

True to its character, the home blurs the line between indoors and out with walls of glass and an extensive covered porch. Views of nature mix with the glow of an inglenook hearth in the leisure room, where family members and close friends can gather.

Two guest suites provide accommodations for visiting relatives and friends. Each of the suites offers a private bath and walk-in closet. A gallery hall connects the suites and leads to a convenient laundry and lower-level staircase. The master wing opens to a private area of the rear covered porch. Nearby, a cabana-style powder room opens to the porch and to the homeowner's private hall. Pocket doors to the study provide a quiet place for reading, surfing and quiet conversations.

## PLAN HPT030058

Total Living Area: 3,074 square feet
Width: 77'-0"
Depth: 66'-8"

# TRANQUILITY AND HAPPINESS

*High style and timeless beauty create an ultra-voguish paradise that is just right for new and traditional neighborhoods.*

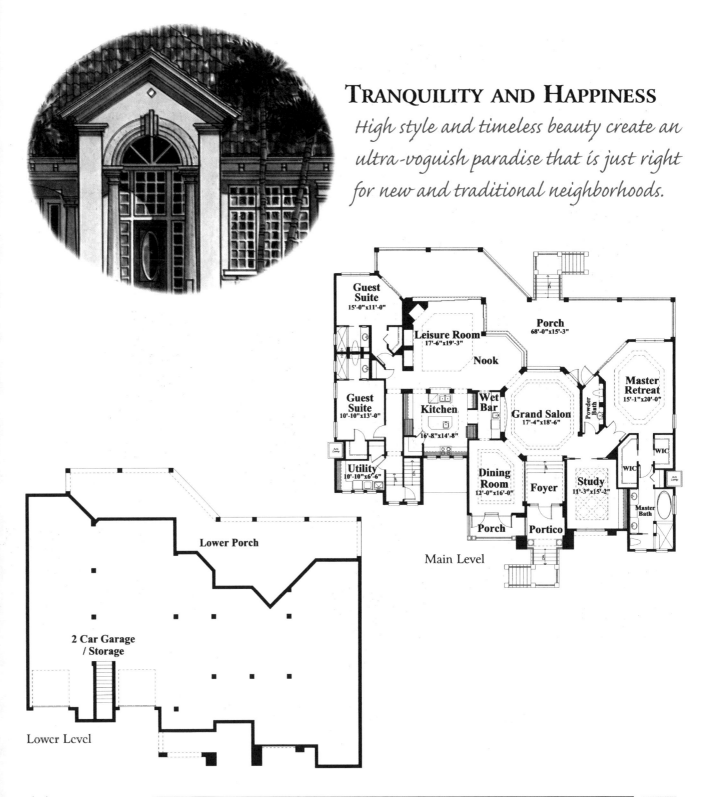

Main Level

Lower Level

Rue Nouveau

This magnificent villa boasts a beautiful stucco exterior, Spanish-tiled roof and Old World details such as arches and accent columns framing the spectacular entry. The striking appeal of the home introduces an interior that revisits the past in glorious style and sets a new standard for comfort and luxury. Open rooms, French doors and vaulted ceilings add an air of spaciousness throughout the home.

The heart of the home is served by a well-crafted kitchen with wrapping counter space and an island cooktop counter. The breakfast nook enjoys a view of the veranda and beyond, and brings natural light to the casual eating space. To the right of the foyer, an open formal dining room provides dazzling views and an ambience of elegance and comfort. Archways supported by columns separate the dining room from the great room, which boasts a fireplace and built-in cabinetry.

On the upper level, the master suite features a sitting area and a private veranda. The private bath provides a knee-space vanity, whirlpool tub and walk-in closet. The lower level offers a three-car garage and bonus space that could be developed as a recreation room.

## PLAN HPT030059

Main Level: 1,671 square feet

Upper Level: 846 square feet

Lower-level Entry: 140 square feet

Total Living Area: 2,657 square feet

Width: 44'-0"

Depth: 55'-0"

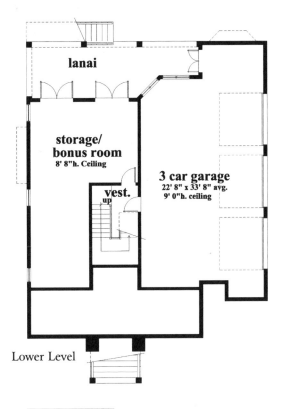

Lower Level

Main Level

## STROKES OF GENIUS

*The graceful curves of a fanlight transom are echoed by classic arches, sweetened by a Mediterranean influence.*

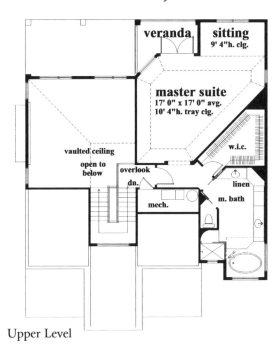

Upper Level

*Sommerset*

An elegant portico and deck enhance the outdoor flow of this enchanting manor, extending the living space and creating a firm connection with nature. Lower-level living spaces open to the outside through a series of stunning French doors. Crafted details such as coffered ceilings and built-in cabinetry underscore the easygoing spirit of the Sun Country.

A gallery-style foyer leads to a powder room and walk-in pantry, which enhances the efficiency of the kitchen. Wrapping counter space provides an overlook to a breakfast bay and 180-degree views of the rear property. A staircase leads up to the magnificent sleeping quarters.

The master bedroom opens to a wrap-around deck—a breezy outdoor retreat fit for reflection or winking at the moon. At the other end of the deck, French doors lead to a quiet study and a loft area spacious enough for computers. Secondary accommodations include a compartmented bath that offers dual lavatories and a private door to each of two bedrooms.

## PLAN HPT030060

Main Level: 1,266 square feet

Upper Level: 1,324 square feet

Total Living Area: 2,590 square feet

Width: 34'-0"

Depth: 63'-2"

# GLOBAL INFLUENCES

*With all the charm of a romantic Mediterranean villa, this artful composition mixes sensational looks with the feeling of home.*

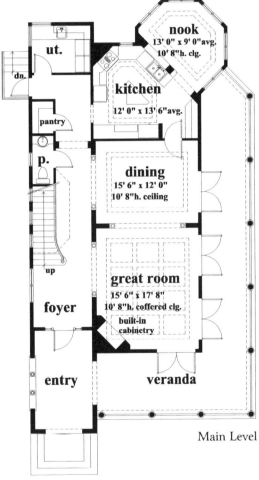

Main Level

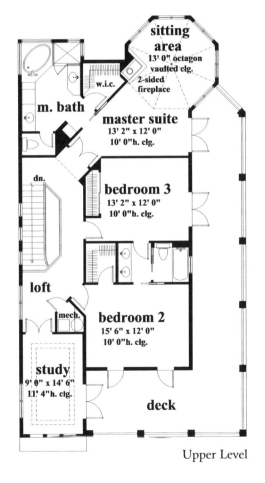

Upper Level

Design © The Sater Group

Terra di Mare

P alatial and practical, this majestic villa radiates with a clean simplicity that will lend a sense of grandeur to any neighborhood. An impressive covered entry and balcony, accented with double columns and a keystone arch, echo the beautiful balustrade of the observation deck.

Sunshine spills into the foyer through an arched transom, sidelights and a pair of French doors that open to a grand staircase leading to the vaulted great room. Interior columns separate rooms and create openness, and a multitude of windows lends views of the covered porch to the rear. The formal dining room boasts an eleven-foot tray ceiling and decorative columns suited for elegant entertaining.

To the left of the plan, each of two clustered secondary bedrooms leads to a private area of the rear porch. The upper level is dedicated to a lavish master suite, which opens to a balcony overlook of the great room. French doors open the homeowner's bedroom to a private porch, where natural views and fresh breezes will invigorate the spirit. Inside, an opulent bath features a dual-sink vanity, whirlpool tub and an oversized shower.

## PLAN HPT030061

Main Level: 1,383 square feet

Upper Level: 595 square feet

Total Living Area: 1,978 square feet

Width: 48'-0"

Depth: 42'-0"

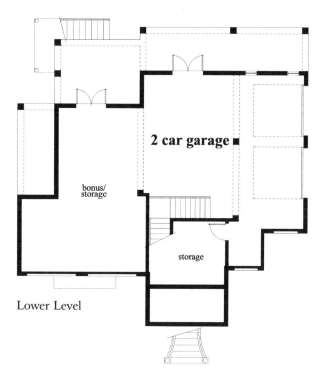

Lower Level

Main Level

# LIVE IT UP

*An enchanting double portico allows a world of views and elegant space just right for bare feet.*

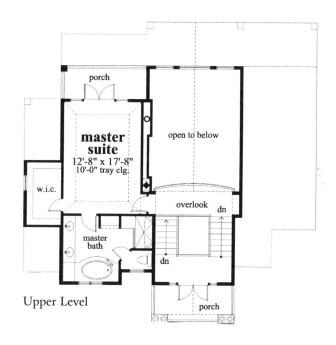

Upper Level

Via Pascoli

Design © The Sater Group

With timeless elements borrowed from the Mediterranean region, this brilliant villa brags one of the best *today* floor plans in the business. The grand balustrade and recessed entry are just the beginning of a truly spectacular home.

A hip vaulted ceiling highlights the great room—a perfect place to entertain, made cozy by a massive fireplace and built-in cabinetry. Decorative columns set this room apart from the morning nook and gallery hall, while French doors open the space to a sheltered porch. An angled snack counter provides an uninterrupted interior vista of the living area from the gourmet kitchen. People will gather here for conversation and on-the-run meals.

On the lower level, separate bonus spaces easily convert to hobby rooms or can be used for additional storage. To the rear of the plan, French doors open to a spacious lanai—a beautiful spot for enjoying the harmonious sounds of the sea. An additional storage area promises room for unused toys and furnishings. Even with a two-car garage, this floor plan is ready for bicycles, golf carts and motorcycles.

## PLAN HPT030062

Total Living Area: 2,137 square feet
Width: 44'-0"
Depth: 61'-0"

# DREAM DREAM

*Perfect proportions create the best-ever dream home with smart amenities and plenty of personality.*

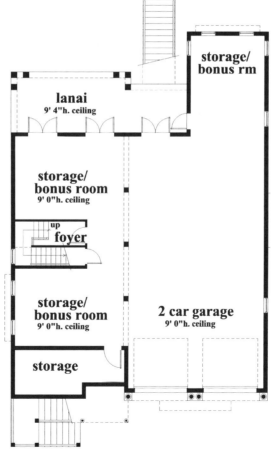

Lower Level

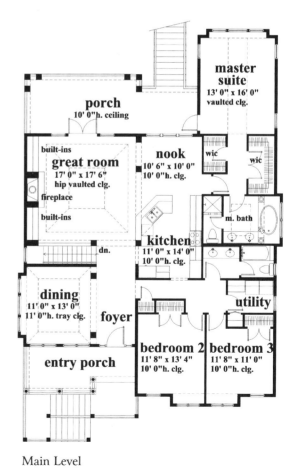

Main Level

Saint Basque

I talian country elegance graces the exterior of this casa bellisima, swept in Mediterranean enchantment. The traditional stucco facade evokes the essence of a distinctly European villa. The covered entryway extends to the foyer, where straight ahead, the two-story great room spaciously enhances the interior. This room features a warming fireplace and offers built-in cabinetry. Double doors open to a romantic veranda, which wraps around to the rear deck.

An open dining room extends through double doors to the veranda on the left side on the plan. The adjacent kitchen features efficient pantry space. A family bedroom with a private bath, a powder room and a utility room also reside on this main floor.

Upstairs, a vaulted master suite with a vaulted owners bath and a private deck share this level with a loft area, which overlooks the great room. Downstairs, the basement-level bonus room and storage area share space with the two-car garage. Two lanais open on either side of the bonus room for additional outdoor patio space.

## PLAN HPT030063

Main Level: 1,143 square feet

Upper Level: 651 square feet

Total Living Area: 1,794 square feet

Width: 32'-0"

Depth: 57'-0"

# THEN AND NOW

*The aesthetic appeal of well-designed buildings takes on the beauty and efficiency of a safe refuge here.*

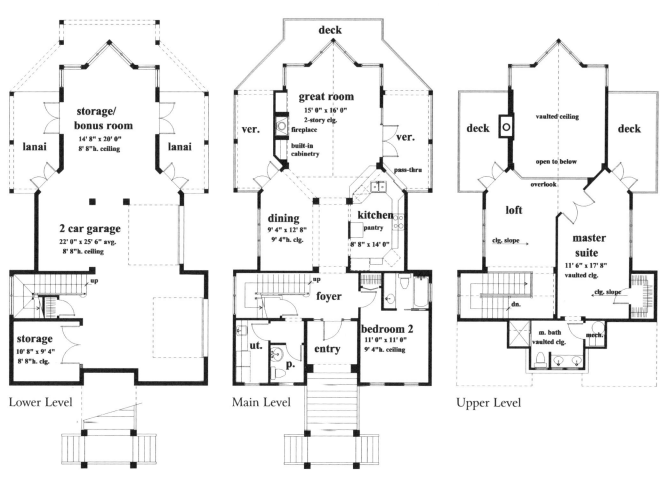

Lower Level

Main Level

Upper Level

## The Blueprint Package

Each set of home plan blueprints is a related gathering of plans, diagrams, measurements, details and specifications that precisely show how your new residence will come together. Each home design receives careful attention and planning from our expert staff to ensure quality and buildability.

**Here's what the package includes:**

- Designer's rendering of front elevation
- Foundation and dimensioned floor plans
- Building cross-sections
- Selected interior elevations
- Working drawings of ¼" scale or larger
- Door and window sizes
- Roof plan and exterior details

☎ **ORDER TOLL FREE 1-800-521-6797**

After you've looked over The Blueprint Package and Important Extras on the following page, simply mail the order form on page 143 or call toll free on our **Blueprint Hotline: 1-800-521-6797 or 520-297-8200.**

**For Customer Service,
Call Toll-free 1-888-690-1116.**

**BLUEPRINTS ARE NOT REFUNDABLE
EXCHANGES ONLY**

**Visit our website:
www.eplans.com**

---

# *Important Extras To Do The Job Right!*

## MATERIALS LIST

For many of the designs in our portfolio, we offer a customized materials take-off that is invaluable in planning and estimating the cost of your new home. This Materials List outlines the quantity, type and size of materials needed to build your house (with the exception of mechanical system items). Included are framing lumber, windows and doors, kitchen and bath cabinetry, rough and finish hardware, and much more. This handy list helps you or your builder cost out materials and serves as a reference sheet when you're compiling bids. A Materials List cannot be ordered before blueprints are ordered.

*(Note: Because of the diversity of local building codes, our Materials List does not include mechanical materials.)*

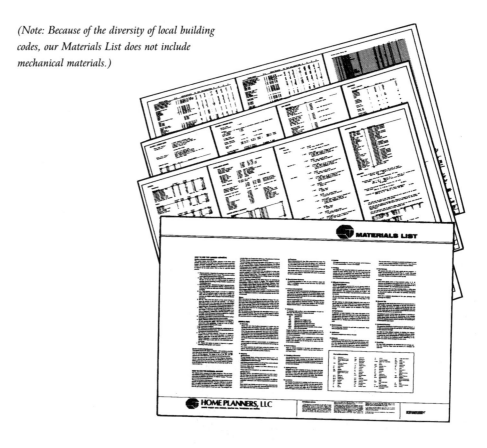

# Construction Information

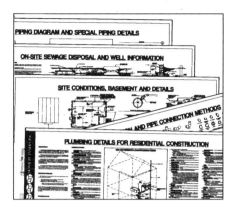

## PLUMBING

The Blueprint Package includes locations for all the plumbing fixtures; however, if you want to know more about the complete plumbing system, these Plumbing Details will prove very useful. Prepared to meet requirements of the National Plumbing Code, these fact-filled sheets give general information on pipe schedules, fittings, sump-pump details, water-softener hookups, septic system details and much more. Sheets also include a glossary of terms.

## ELECTRICAL

The locations for every electrical switch, plug and outlet are shown in your Blueprint Package. However, these Electrical Details go further to take the mystery out of household electrical systems. Prepared to meet requirements of the National Electrical Code, these comprehensive drawings come packed with helpful information, including wire sizing, switch-installation schematics and much more.

## CONSTRUCTION

The Blueprint Package contains everything an experienced builder needs to construct a particular house. However, it doesn't show all the ways that houses can be built, nor does it explain alternate construction methods. To help you understand how your house will be built—and offer additional techniques—this set of Construction Details depicts the materials and methods used to build foundations, fireplaces, walls, floors and roofs.

## MECHANICAL

These Mechanical Details contain fundamental principles and useful data that will help you make informed decisions and communicate with subcontractors about heating and cooling systems. Drawings contain instructions and samples that allow you to make simple load calculations, and preliminary sizing and costing analysis. The package is filled with illustrations and diagrams to help you visualize components and how they relate to one another.

## SPECIFICATION OUTLINE

This valuable 16-page document is critical to building your house correctly. Designed to be filled in by you or your builder, this book lists 166 stages or items crucial to the building process. It provides a comprehensive review of the construction process and helps in choosing of materials. When combined with the blueprints, a signed contract, and a schedule, it becomes a legal document and record for the building of your home.

## 11"x17" COLOR RENDERING

Full-color renderings suitable for framing are available for all of the plans contained in this book. For prices and additional information, please see page 140 or call the toll-free number listed below.

## ☎ To Order, Call Toll Free 1-800-521-6797

To add these important extras to your Blueprint Package, simply indicate your choices on the order form on page 143 or call us Toll Free 1-800-521-6797.

# House Blueprint Price Schedule

(Prices guaranteed through December 31, 2001)

| Tier | 1-set Study Package | 4-set Building Package | 8-set Building Package | Sepia Package |
|------|------|------|------|------|
| A3 | 500 | 540 | 600 | 745 |
| A4 | 540 | 580 | 640 | 805 |
| C1 | 585 | 625 | 685 | 870 |
| C2 | 625 | 665 | 725 | 930 |
| C3 | 675 | 715 | 775 | 980 |
| C4 | 725 | 765 | 825 | 1,030 |
| L1 | 785 | 825 | 885 | 1,090 |
| L2 | 835 | 875 | 935 | 1,140 |

Prices for 4 or 8-set Building Packages honored only at time of original order. One-set study packages are marked "not for construction."

Additional Identical Blueprints in same order:
"A3–L2" price plans..................................................................$50 per set

Reverse Blueprints with 4- or 8-set order for "A3–L2" price plans...$50 fee per order

Specification Outlines.............................................................$10 each

Materials Lists for "A3–C3" price plans .............................$60 each

Materials Lists for "C4–L2" price plans .............................$70 each

11"x17" Color Rendering, Front Perspective ......................$100

Set of Front and Rear Perspectives ....................................$175
(Rear Perspectives are available on Mount Julian and Santa Rosa plans only.)

All items, prices, terms and conditions are subject to change without notice and subject to availability. Reversed plans are mirror-image sets with lettering and dimensioning shown backwards. To receive plans in reverse, specifically request this when placing your order. Since lettering and dimensions appear backward on reverse blueprints, we suggest you order one set reversed for siting and the rest as shown for construction purposes. *Reproducible vellums are granted with a non-exclusive license to make up to twelve (12) copies for use in the construction of a single home.*

Plans are designed to specifications published by the Southern Building Code Congress (SBCCI) International, Inc. or the Building Officials and Code Administrators (BOCA). Our plans are designed to meet or exceed national building standards. Because of the great differences in geography and climate throughout the United States and Canada, each state, country and municipality has its own building codes, zone requirements, ordinances and building regulations. Your plan may need to be modified to comply with local requirements regarding snow loads, energy codes, soil and seismic conditions and a wide range of other matters. In addition, you may need to obtain permits or inspections from local governments before and in the course of construction. Prior to using blueprints ordered from us, we strongly advise that you consult a licensed architect or engineer—and speak with your local building official—before applying for any permit or beginning construction. We authorize the use of our blueprints on the express condition that you strictly comply with all local building codes, zoning requirements and other applicable laws, regulations, ordinances and requirements. **Notice: Plans for homes to be built in Nevada must be re-drawn by a Nevada-registered professional. Consult your building official for more information on this subject.**

# Index

To use the Index below, refer to the design name and price code listed (a helpful page reference is also given). Refer to the Price Schedule for the cost of one, four or eight sets of blueprints or the cost of a reproducible sepia. Additional prices are shown for identical and reverse blueprint sets.

**To Order:** Fill in and send the order form on page 143—or call toll free 1-800-521-6797 or 520-297-8200.

For Customer Service, please call 1-888-690-1116.

| Plan Name | Plan Number | Price Code | Page | Alternate Elevations |
|---|---|---|---|---|
| Hyatt Park | HPT030045 | L2 | 100 | 48, 66 |
| Jupiter Bay | HPT030044 | L2 | 98 | 36, 98 |
| Key Largo | HPT030038 | C3 | 84 | 30, 130 |
| La Palma | HPT030029 | L2 | 66 | 48, 100 |
| Laguna Beach | HPT030040 | C1 | 88 | 24, 102 |
| Lake Tahoe | HPT030013 | C3 | 32 | 58, 116 |
| Laurel Ridge | HPT030001 | L1 | 8 | 76, 110 |
| Les Anges | HPT030026 | C4 | 60 | 42, 122 |
| Linden Place | HPT030024 | C2 | 56 | 12, 114 |
| Mimosa | HPT030032 | C4 | 72 | 46, 126 |
| Mission Hills | HPT030043 | A4 | 96 | 44, 80 |
| Montego Bay | HPT030022 | C3 | 52 | 16, 112 |
| Monterrey Cove | HPT030028 | C3 | 64 | 20, 124 |
| Montserrat | HPT030031 | C1 | 70 | 40, 104 |
| Mount Julian | HPT030011 | A3 | 28 | 92, 136 |
| Mount Whitney | HPT030020 | C4 | 46 | 72, 126 |
| New Waterford | HPT030012 | C3 | 30 | 84, 130 |
| Newport Cove | HPT030041 | A4 | 90 | 14, 134 |
| Nicholas Park | HPT030052 | C2 | 114 | 12, 56 |
| Papillon | HPT030035 | C2 | 78 | 34, 118 |
| Plymouth Bay | HPT030042 | A3 | 92 | 28, 136 |
| Riviera dei Fiori | HPT030053 | C3 | 116 | 32, 58 |
| Royal Marco | HPT030047 | C1 | 104 | 40, 70 |
| Rue Nouveau | HPT030059 | C3 | 128 | 18, 82 |
| Saint Basque | HPT030063 | A3 | 136 | 28, 92 |
| Saint Croix | HPT030030 | L2 | 68 | 36, 98 |
| Saint Martin | HPT030036 | A4 | 80 | 44, 96 |
| San Marino | HPT030046 | C1 | 102 | 24, 88 |
| Santa Rosa | HPT030023 | C1 | 54 | 10, 132 |
| Savona Cove | HPT030034 | L1 | 76 | 8, 110 |
| Sierra Canyon | HPT030015 | L2 | 36 | 68, 98 |
| Sommerset | HPT030060 | C3 | 130 | 30, 84 |
| Stone Bridge | HPT030007 | C3 | 20 | 64, 124 |
| Sunset Beach | HPT030049 | C1 | 108 | 38, 74 |
| Terra di Mare | HPT030061 | C1 | 132 | 10, 54 |
| Trail Ridge | HPT030019 | A4 | 44 | 80, 96 |
| Via Pascoli | HPT030062 | A4 | 134 | 14, 90 |
| Villa Caprini | HPT030055 | A3 | 120 | 26, 86 |
| Villa Tucano | HPT030050 | L1 | 110 | 8, 76 |
| Walden Hill | HPT030003 | C2 | 12 | 56, 114 |
| Wedgewood | HPT030008 | A3 | 22 | 62, 106 |
| Weymouth Inn | HPT030016 | C3 | 38 | 74, 108 |
| Whisperwood | HPT030004 | A4 | 14 | 90, 134 |
| Wolf Summit | HPT030018 | C4 | 42 | 60, 122 |

# Before You Order...

Before filling out the coupon at right or calling us on our Toll-Free Blueprint Hotline, you may want to learn more about our services and products. Here's some information you will find helpful.

## Our Exchange Policy

Since blueprints are printed in response to your order, we cannot honor requests for refunds. However, we will exchange your entire first order for an equal or greater number of blueprints within our plan collection within 90 days of the original order. The entire content of your original order must be returned to our offices before an exchange will be processed. If the returned blueprints look used, redlined or copied, we will not honor your exchange. Fees for exchanging your blueprints are as follows: 20% of the amount of the original order...*plus* the difference in cost if exchanging for a design in a higher price bracket or *less* the difference in cost if exchanging for a design in lower price bracket. **(Reproducible blueprints are not exchangeable.)** Please add $25 for postage and handling via Regular Service; $35 via Priority Service; $45 via Express Service. Shipping and handling charges are not refundable.

## About Reverse Blueprints

If you want to build in reverse of the plan as shown, we will include an extra set of reverse blueprints (mirror image) for an additional fee of $50. Although lettering and dimensions will appear backward, reverse will be a useful aid if you decide to flop the plan. To receive plans in reverse, specifically request this when placing your order. Since lettering and dimensions appear backward on reverse blueprints, we suggest you order one set reversed for siting and the rest as shown for construction purposes. Reproducible vellums are granted with a non-exclusive license to make up to twelve (12) copies for use in the construction of a single home.

## Revising, Modifying and Customizing Plans

The wide variety of designs available in this publication allows you to select ideas and concepts for a home to fit your building site and match your family's needs, wants and budget. Like many homeowners who buy these plans, you and your builder, architect or engineer may want to make changes to them. Your builder may make some minor changes, but we recommend that a licensed architect or engineer make most changes. As set forth below, we cannot assume any responsibility for blueprints that have been changed, whether by you, your builder or by professionals selected by you or referred to you by us, because such individuals are outside our supervision and control. Any modifications made to the vellums by parties other than The Sater Group voids any warranties express or implied including the warranties of fitness for a particular purpose and merchantability.

## Architectural and Engineering Seals

Some cities and states are now requiring that a licensed architect or engineer review and seal a blueprint, or officially approve it, prior to construction due to concerns over energy costs, safety and other factors. Prior to application for a building permit or the start of actual construction, we strongly advise that you consult your local building official who can tell you if such a review is required.

## Local Building codes and Zoning Requirements

Plans are designed to specifications published by the Southern Building Code Congress (SBCCI) International Inc. or the Building Officials and Code Administrators (BOCA). Our plans are designed to meet or exceed national building standards. Because of the great differences in geography and climate throughout the United States and Canada, each state, country and municipality has its own building codes, zone requirements, ordinances and building regulations. Your plan may need to be modified to comply with local requirements regarding snow loads, energy codes, soil and seismic conditions and a wide range of other matters. In addition, you may need to obtain permits or inspections from local governments before and in the course of construction. Prior to using blueprints ordered from us, we strongly advise that you consult a licensed architect or engineer—and speak with your local building official—before applying for any permit or beginning construction. We authorize the use of our blueprints on the express condition that you strictly comply with all local building codes, zoning requirements and other applicable laws, regulations, ordinances and requirements. **Notice: Plans for homes to build in Nevada must be re-drawn by a Nevada-registered professional. Consult your building official for more information on this subject.**

## Disclaimer

Substantial care and effort has gone into the creation of these blueprints. However, because we cannot provide on-site consultation, supervision and control over actual construction, and because of the great variance in local building requirements, building practices and soil, seismic, weather and other conditions, WE CANNOT MAKE ANY WARRANTY, EXPRESS OR IMPLIED, WITH RESPECT TO THE CONTENT OR USE OF OUR BLUEPRINTS, INCLUDING BUT NOT LIMITED TO ANY WARRANTY OR MERCHANTABILITY OR OF FITNESS FOR A PARTICULAR PURPOSE. **Items, prices, terms and conditions are subject to change without notice.**

## Terms and Conditions

These designs are protected under the terms of United States Copyright Law and may not be copied or reproduced in any way, by any means, unless you have purchased Sepias or Reproducibles which clearly indicate your right to copy or reproduce. We authorize the use of your chosen design as an aid in the construction on one single-family home only. You may not use this design to build a second or multiple dwellings without purchasing another blueprint or blueprints or paying additional design fees. The title to and intellectual property rights in the plans shall remain with The Sater Group. Use of the plans in a manner inconsistent with this agreement is a violation of U.S. Copyright laws. Additional sets of the same plan may be ordered within a 60-day period at $50 each, plus shipping and tax, if applicable. After 60 days, re-orders are treated as new orders.

## How Many Blueprints Do You Need?

A single set of blueprints is sufficient to study a home in great detail. However, if you are planning to obtain cost estimates from a contractor or subcontractors—or if you are planning to build immediately—you will need more sets. Because additional sets are cheaper when ordering quantity with the original order, make sure you order enough blueprints to satisfy all requirements. The following checklist will help you determine how many you will need:

___ Owner

___ Builder (generally requires at least three sets; one as a legal document, one to use during inspections, and at least one to give to subcontractors)

___ Local Building Department (often requires two sets)

___ Mortgage Lender (usually one set for a conventional loan; three sets for FHA or VA loans)

___ TOTAL NUMBER OF SETS

## Toll Free 1-800-521-6797 or 520-297-8200

 Regular Office Hours:
8:00 a.m. to 10:00 p.m. EST, Monday through Friday
10:00 a.m.-7:00 p.m. EST Saturday and Sunday

Our staff will gladly answer any questions during regular office hours. Our answering service can place orders after hours or on weekends.

If we receive your order by 4:00 p.m. Eastern Time, Monday through Friday, we'll process it and ship within 48 hours. When ordering by phone, please have your charge card ready. We'll also ask you for the Order Form Key Number at the bottom of the coupon.

By FAX: Copy the order form on the next page and send it on our FAX line: 1-800-224-6699 or 1-520-544-3086.

### Browse our website:
### www.eplans.com

## Canadian Customers Order Toll-Free 1-877-223-6389

For faster service and plans that are modified for building in Canada, customers may now call in orders directly to our Canadian supplier of plans and charge the purchase to a charge card. Or, you may complete the order form at right, adding 40% to all prices and mail in Canadian funds to:

**Home Planners Canada
c/o Select Home Designs**
301-611 Alexander Street
Vancouver C, Canada V6A 1E1

**OR:** Copy the Order Form and send it via our Canadian FAX line: 1-800-224-6699

## BLUEPRINTS ARE NOT REFUNDABLE EXCHANGES ONLY

---

## ORDER FORM

HOME PLANNERS, LLC
Wholly owned by Hanley-Wood, LLC
3275 WEST INA ROAD, SUITE 110
TUCSON, ARIZONA 85741

*Call for current pricing and availability prior to mailing this order form.*

### THE BASIC BLUEPRINT PACKAGE
Rush me the following (Please refer to the Plans Index and Price Schedule on pages 140-141):
___ Set(s) of Blueprints for Plan Number(s)_____.                                    $_____
___ Set(s) of Reproducible Sepia(s)_____.                                              $_____
___ Additional Identical Blueprints in same order:
   A3-L2 price plans @ $50 per set.                                        $_____
___ Reverse Blueprints (mirror image):
   with 4- or 8-set order for A3–L2 price plans @ $50 fee per order.        $_____

### ADDITIONAL PRODUCTS
Rush me the following:
___ 11"x17" Color Rendering(s) for Plan Number(s)_____.                               $_____
___ Specification Outlines @$10 each.                                                  $_____
___ Materials List: $60 each for A3-C3 price plans; $70 each for C4-L2 price plans
   (Must be purchased with Blueprint set)                                 $_____
___ Detail Sets @$14.95 each; any two for $22.95; any three
   for $29.95; all four for $39.95 (Save $19.85).                         $_____
   ___Plumbing___Electrical___Construction___Mechanical
   (These helpful details provide general construction advice and are not specific to any single plan.)

| POSTAGE AND HANDLING | 1-3 sets | 4 or more sets |
|---|---|---|
| • Regular Service (Allow 7-10 days delivery) | $20.00 | $25.00 |
| • Priority (Allow 4-5 days delivery) | $25.00 | $35.00 |
| • Express (Allow 3 days delivery) | $35.00 | $45.00 |

OVERSEAS DELIVERY: Fax, phone or mail for quote

*NOTE: All delivery times are from date Blueprint Package is shipped.*

POSTAGE (From box above)                                                                $_____
SUBTOTAL                                                                                $_____
SALES TAX (AZ and MI residents please add appropriate
       state & local sales tax.)                      $_____
TOTAL (Subtotal and Tax)                                                                $_____
YOUR ADDRESS (Please print) (Street address required)
Name _____
Street _____
City_____State_____Zip_____
Daytime telephone number (____) _____

FOR CREDIT CARD ORDERS ONLY Please fill in the information below:
Credit card number_____
Exp. Date: Month/Year _____
Check one  ❏ Visa    ❏ MasterCard    ❏ Discover Card    ❏ American Express
Signature_____
Please check appropriate box:  ❏ Licensed Builder-Contractor
               ❏ Homeowner

Order Form Key

HPT03

## Cabins, Cottages & Villas

*Designed by Matthew S. Kauffman*
*Set in Arrus and Caflisch Script*
*Illustrated by Dave Jenkins*
*Printed by Davidson Printing Company on Nekoosa Feltweave*